Car of the Year
1895–1970

Henry B. Lent

CAR OF THE YEAR

1895-1970 A 75-Year Parade

of American Automobiles That Made News

E. P. DUTTON & CO., INC. NEW YORK

COPY 12

Library of Congress Catalog Card Number: 70–102745
SBN 0-525-27451-0

Contents

Foreword

More than seventy-five fabulous years have passed since America's first horseless carriage chuffed and chugged down a street in Springfield, Massachusetts. Yet even by the turn of the century, when more and more of the odd-looking contraptions began to appear, most people thought they were just a passing fad.

There are men still living who remember their boyhood days when groups of amused bystanders used to jeer, "Get a horse!" if they saw an embarrassed driver struggling with the crank of his balky little one-cylinder gas buggy in an effort to get it going again. In those days, anyone who was silly enough to predict that the automobile was the coming thing was regarded as a crackpot, in a class with those who talked of someday flying to the moon on a rocket.

Luckily for all of us, the skeptics and the scoffers turned out to be mistaken—and the pioneer auto makers were right. Most of them lived to see America become a nation on wheels because of the automobiles they invented and built.

Few material things have been more important than the automobile in shaping our lives, our industrial growth, and our national economy. And whether we realize it or not, few material things have become more deeply rooted in our hearts and our emotions. We cherish the early cars because they recall an era and a simple way of life long past. So do the glorious classic cars that followed them. Just as surely, the gleaming creations that appeared from the mid-century to the present day have become symbols of a modern way of life we couldn't change even if we wanted to.

All of them, from the valiant veterans of yesterday to the sleek cars of our own times, have a story that deserves to be told.

This book is an attempt to tell part of that story, as well as the story of some of the men who did so much to make the great American dream come true. It is not, by any means, a complete history of the American automobile. The cars shown on these pages are just a few of the more than sixteen hundred different makes of automobiles that helped bring about vast changes in the American scene over the past seventy-five years.

Except for the war years, when the military Jeep was the only automobile produced, I have chosen a single car for each year from 1895 to 1970. Each automobile included in my collection has been chosen because of my own personal feelings about the car. I have also selected each "car of the year" because, in my opinion, it was newsworthy for one reason or another.

It would be strange indeed if everyone who happens to read this book agrees with all my selections. Strange? It would be a miracle! After all, when yesterday's Mercer and Stutz Bearcat owners fiercely defended the relative merits of the two cars, and the driver of today's Camaro looks with dismay on a friend who happens to prefer a Mustang, who would be brash enough to set himself up as the last word on such a controversial subject as the great American automobile?

There has been many a year between 1895 and 1970 when a dozen or more different automobiles earned the right to be counted among the truly "great" ones. So, in compiling this car-of-the-year collection, it was necessary to omit many of the grand old marques that surely deserved to be included, and some of the glamorous newer cars that were equally exciting.

To the many individuals who helped me write the book and provided photographs of the automobiles, I am deeply grateful. My friends on the public relations staffs of the major automobile companies never failed to respond to my continuing requests for information and technical data: Bill Adams of General Motors, Jerry Rideout of Buick, Jack White of Oldsmobile, Myron Scott of Chevrolet, Howard Hendricks of Chrysler, Bob Fuehrer of Ford, Murray Stahl of Kaiser Jeep, and John Conde of American Motors.

A special note of thanks to two friends and car buffs in Woodstock, Vermont: C. P. ("Perce") Weldon, who willingly, and often, pored through his automotive archives to dig up needed data, and Curt Gerrish, who offered a number of helpful suggestions.

From Frank H. Gardner and Raymond Washburn, of the Antique Auto Museum in Brookline, Massachusetts, came more information eagerly sought, as well as from Everett M. Dickinson, publisher of the veteran car owners' magazine, *The Bulb Horn*, and editor Walter MacIlvain, who gave me interesting facts about such old-time cars as the Peerless, Lozier, Owen Magnetic, and Kissel . . . Don H. Berkebile of the Smithsonian Institution . . . Frank Taylor, editor of *Car Classics* magazine . . . Miss Susan Hager of the Raymond Loewy/William Snaith automotive design studios . . . Bernard J. Weiss of the Pierce-Arrow Society, and Major Herbert M. Dawley, former Pierce-Arrow stylist . . . Julian L. Watkins, author of the classic book, *The 100 Greatest Advertisements*, for the Jordan Playboy story . . . L. Scott Bailey, editor and publisher of the elegant *Automobile Quarterly*, and his assistant, Miss Carol N. Wolfson . . . Dr. Robert C. Lusk, of Detroit's Automobile Manufacturers Association . . . Henry E. Edmunds, of the Henry Ford Museum in Dearborn . . . Henry Austin Clark, Jr., of the Long Island Automotive Museum . . . and James T. Bradley, head of the Detroit Public Library's famed Automotive History Collection.

Because of their help, I hope you will find this book as much fun and as interesting to read as it was for me to write.

Car of the Year
1895–1970

Thanksgiving Day, 1895, turned out to be a red-letter day for the pioneer American automobile builder, Frank Duryea. On that day, a gas buggy built by the newly formed Duryea Motor Wagon Company was entered in the first official automobile race ever held in this country.

The car was one of eleven different machines that were scheduled to make the run from Chicago to Evanston and back, a total distance of 54 miles. Frank Duryea, seated at the tiller of his rugged little 2-cylinder car, beat them all and won the $2,000 prize awarded by the Chicago *Times-Herald,* the newspaper that sponsored the race.

The weather that day was bitterly cold and blustery. The course was covered by windblown snow. The engines of several of the cars balked and refused to run. Their owners never got beyond the starting line. The three electric automobiles entered in the race didn't get very far. Their wheels, spinning on the slippery road, used up so much current that their batteries ran down. One by one, the remaining cars dropped out of the race—all of them except the Duryea and a German-built Benz. The Duryea, tooling along at a steady 7½mph, passed its foreign rival on the home stretch and sped on to victory. It completed the grueling daylong run at 7:10 that evening, almost two hours before the Benz limped in across the finish line. The race of these pioneer automobiles made big news across the country.

Frank Duryea and his brother Charles had made even bigger news two years before this, when they wheezed along the main street of Springfield, Massachusetts, in a strange contraption they had just invented—the first successful gasoline-powered vehicle ever built in America.

This first Duryea was actually a light, high-wheeled carriage with a small 1-cylinder, 4hp engine mounted horizontally at the rear, underneath the body. Tiller-steered, it had all the regulation trimmings of a horse-drawn carriage, including a buggylike top and leather dash, a pair of oil lamps, and a whipsocket. It was propelled by a simple belt-and-pulley arrangement between the engine and a pair of large sprockets bolted to the wood spokes on the inner side of the iron-rimmed rear wheels. There was a little crank at the back of the car for starting the engine.

On its trial run, America's first horseless carriage sputtered along at a brisk speed of 10mph. Some of the townsfolk who saw it shook their heads in wonderment over this latest caper of the "crazy" Duryea brothers, unaware that they were that day witnessing an event that would eventually change their lives beyond all imagination.

The 1893 Duryea, the great-great-granddaddy of millions of American automobiles to follow, now occupies a place of honor in the collection of antique cars in the Museum of the Smithsonian Institution. Be sure to see it the next time you are in Washington, D.C.

1896/ *Ford Quadricycle*

Like many other Michigan farm boys, Henry Ford had always had a knack for things mechanical. As a youngster, his pet hobby was tinkering with old clocks and watches. So when he grew up, no one was surprised to hear that he had left the farm and had landed a job as engineer with the Detroit electric light company.

But how does a grown-up country boy manage to keep on tinkering and inventing things when he gets a job in the city? This one solved the problem by persuading his landlord to let him fix up a workshop in a small shed that was located behind the two-family house in which he lived. Here he spent every hour he could, day and night, experimenting with gasoline engines and trying to build an automobile that would really run.

One day in the spring of 1896, the landlord heard a terrific racket coming from the direction of the shed. Rushing out, he found that his tenant had just finished knocking a big opening in the side of the building so that he could roll out his new invention. "It's too wide to go through the door," he explained apologetically.

His landlord was so amazed at the sight of the extraordinary contraption that instead of being angry with young Ford, he gave him a helping hand in pushing it out onto the street. Then, when its inventor had clambered aboard, he kept on pushing, for he was told that was the way to start the engine. After a few hesitant pops, the engine caught hold and the vehicle chugged away down Bagley Avenue on its trial run.

In those days, nobody knew what an automobile was supposed to look like. This one, they agreed, seemed to be only a small buckboard mounted on 4 bicycle wheels, with a dinky little 2-cylinder horizontal engine bolted to the frame in back of the driver. It had no steering wheel, no brakes, no reverse gear. It was actually a belt-driven gas buggy, with a choice of 2 forward speeds. There was a tiller for steering, a 3-gallon fuel tank under the seat, and a bicycle bell attached to the front of the dash to warn unwary pedestrians of their impending doom. That was the whole package. Top speed, with the engine wide open: 17mph. Henry Ford called his wonderful invention a quadricycle.

Today the quadricycle is on display as a permanent exhibit in the Henry Ford Museum in Dearborn, Michigan. Many of the thousands of visitors who stop each year to view the unique vehicle can scarcely believe their eyes when they learn that they are looking at the world's first Ford automobile.

1897/ *Stanley Steamer*

Everybody in Newton, Massachusetts, knew the Stanley brothers, at least by sight. But few people—even those who worked in their shop—could tell them apart, for they were identical twins. The only difference between them was their middle initial. Mr. F.E. and Mr. F.O. always dressed alike, wore the same kind of derby hat, and even trimmed their beards the same way.

They started in business by making the first violins to be manufactured commercially in this country. Then they invented a generator that ran on illuminating gas, as well as early forms of X-ray equipment. When photography was still in its infancy, they invented a photographic dry plate, later selling this profitable business to Eastman Kodak for a handsome sum.

Now free to devote their time and skills to an idea that had long intrigued them, they set to work building a vehicle that would travel faster than a horse and buggy. In 1897 they completed it—their first steam automobile.

It was a neat little buggy with few moving parts. A firepot under its copper boiler generated steam for the perky steam engine, which was connected to the rear axle by a chain drive. The car had no gearbox. To increase its road speed, you simply moved a hand throttle that controlled the amount of steam admitted to the engine.

One day, to demonstrate what the car could do, Brother F.O. drove a Stanley Steamer up the steep 10-mile gravel road to the summit of Mount Washington, with his wife perched on the high seat beside him. The amazing 2-hour climb made newspaper headlines around the world.

Stanley Steamers were noted for their smooth, quiet power—and their speed. In 1906, the brothers built a steam racing-car, named the Rocket, that was clocked at an incredible speed of 127mph in Ormond, Florida. On a subsequent run, it hit some sand ripples on the beach and "took off like an airplane," according to its driver, who miraculously escaped injury in the spectacular crash.

From year to year, Stanley Steamers were steadily improved, becoming bigger and more luxurious. The line soon included smart runabouts, handsome touring cars, limousines, and a big 12-passenger "mountain wagon" that resembled an open bus.

One of the steam automobile's chief drawbacks was the fact that it took about 15 minutes to get up a head of steam in a cold boiler. And on trips, the driver had to stop every now and then at a convenient horse trough or farmhouse well to refill his boiler.

At one time there were more than 125 different makes of steam automobiles in the United States. But the more efficient gasoline engine finally won out. So, in spite of its glorious past, the future of the elegant Stanley Steamer evaporated in a puff of steam in 1925, when the last one was built. But hundreds of them still exist in perfect running condition, and are proudly displayed at steam-car meets held in various parts of the country every year by the 1,100 members of the Steam Automobile Club of America.

1898 / *Winton*

In the 1880s, a young ocean-steamship engineer named Alexander Winton, who had migrated to this country from his native Scotland, settled in Cleveland, where he soon gained a reputation as a manufacturer of fine bicycles.

Winton's business grew and prospered. But it wasn't long before he began spending more and more of his time experimenting with gasoline engines. He was convinced that the day would come when the bicycle would be replaced by that newfangled contraption people laughingly called the "horseless carriage." Eager to get in on the ground floor as a maker of gas buggies, he put together several experimental models. But no one seemed very interested in them.

Being a stubborn Scot, he didn't give up. In order to show everyone that he meant business, he got some money together and started a new company. He called it the Winton Motor Carriage Company.

The first motor carriage he built, in 1898, was a big success. It was powered by a 1-cylinder, water-cooled, horizontal engine. The buggy had a chain drive, a tiller for steering, 2 forward speeds, and reverse. To start the engine, you inserted a hand crank into a hole on the side of the body and onto a geared shaft.

Winton No. 1 was purchased by a man from Pennsylvania—the first recorded sale of a gasoline-powered vehicle in America. The factory immediately started building 25 more cars just like it. Selling them was no problem, even at $1,000 each,

especially after Alexander Winton demonstrated how dependable his cars were by driving one of them from Cleveland to New York in the incredibly short time of 9 days. His actual running time on this 800-mile endurance run was 78 hours and 43 minutes.

Not satisfied with becoming a pioneer builder of passenger automobiles, Winton set out to make a name for himself as a pioneer hot rodder, too. In one of his racing cars, the 4-cylinder Bullet No. 1, he established speed records that were remarkable for that day: 55.38mph on a horse racetrack in Cleveland, and 68.96mph at Daytona Beach in Florida. Then he built an even faster car, the Bullet No. 2—one of the first automobiles to have an 8-cylinder, in-line engine. Its power plant consisted of two 4-cylinder engines bolted together, with the cylinders lying in a horizontal position. At Daytona Beach, with the famous race driver Barney Oldfield at the wheel, Bullet No. 2 covered a mile in 43 seconds. Its speed of 83.7mph was very close to the world's record then for gasoline-powered automobiles.

Winton automobiles were among the best American cars ever built in the first quarter-century. But in 1924, their maker chose to discontinue producing them so that he could devote his full time to his newest venture, the manufacture of diesel engines.

Winton No. 1, Bullet No. 1, and Bullet No. 2 are on display today in the Smithsonian Museum exhibit in Washington, D.C.

1899/ *Packard*

According to one of history's many automobile legends, the twelfth vehicle built by Alexander Winton was bought on September 13, 1898, by an Ohio electrical goods manufacturer named James Ward Packard.

Young Packard took delivery of his new Winton at the factory in Cleveland and started out for his home in Warren, a distance of about 50 miles. The car broke down several times during the trip. Its engine overheated. A driving chain snapped. Three of its 4 tires blew out. Its disgruntled owner, caked with mud, made the last few miles of the trip home behind a team of horses a sympathetic farmer had hitched to his car.

Several days later, he patiently coaxed the automobile back to the factory. Confronting the great Alexander Winton himself, he complained about its shortcomings and offered a few words of advice on how it could be made a better car. Mr. Winton heard him out, with growing impatience. Then he snapped, "Young man, if you're so smart, why don't you make an automobile yourself?"

"You know, Mr. Winton," Packard replied, "I believe I will."

Having obtained a college degree in mechanical engineering, he was confident he could do it. He enlisted the help of his brother, William, and two friends who shared his fondness for machinery. They promptly set to work in a shed that was attached to the Packard electrical plant.

On November 9, 1899, the first Packard automobile was completed and ready to go. Its proud inventor started the engine. The gas buggy, popping and sputtering, eased out onto the street under its own power, frightening passing horses as well as townspeople who happened to be strolling by as the historic event took place.

Packard called his first automobile the Model A. The perky little machine had bicycle-type wire wheels, a single upholstered seat, and a regular buggy dash. There was a tiller for steering. The 12hp "one-lunger" horizontal engine was bolted to the frame under the seat. Chain-driven, from the gear-box to the rear axle, the automobile boasted 3 forward speeds and reverse.

During the next few years, Packard built and sold several hundred automobiles. Meanwhile, the rivalry between the two pioneer companies continued. Seeking publicity which would give him an edge over his upstart competitor, Winton caused a sensation by staging a cross-country endurance run. In May, 1903, one of his cars was driven from San Francisco to New York in 64 days. Not to be outdone, Packard duplicated the feat with one of his Model F cars, which he dubbed Old Pacific. He succeeded in lopping 3 days off Winton's coast-to-coast running time.

Packards were excellent automobiles right from the start. These early models marked the origin of a company that was to become known the world over, year after year, for its elegant, luxurious automobiles.

1900 / *Riker Piano-Box Electric Runabout*

At the turn of the century, more than one-third of the vehicles being built in the United States were electrics. This neat Piano-Box Runabout was one of them. It had a speed of 14mph and could travel about 25 miles before its batteries required recharging.

It was built by Abraham Lawrence Riker, who had been a prosperous manufacturer of electric fans in Elizabethport, New Jersey. Other models put out by the newly formed Riker Motor Vehicle Company included big motor-driven delivery vans and wagons for department stores and wholesale warehouses.

The oddest vehicle of all was a luxurious but bulky coach, which is now preserved in the Smithsonian Museum. Its enclosed wooden body accommodated 4 passengers, who sat on facing seats. Except for the location of the driver's seat, the vehicle looked very much like the stagecoaches that rumble into Dodge City in today's Old West dramas on TV. The driver and the "footman" of the electric coach sat side by side on a high seat *behind* the body, over the battery compartment. From this precarious perch they could see the road ahead by peering over the roof of the coach. Steering was by tiller, which controlled a vertical shaft connected to a gear on the rear end of a long horizontal shaft that ran underneath the body to the front axle.

Although electric automobiles showed great promise back in 1900, there was doubt in many minds as to which was the best method of powering a horseless carriage. The temperamental gasoline engine was being used by more and more auto makers, although some motorists predicted, "You'll never find many people who want to sit on top of an explosion." Others liked steam automobiles best. For a long time, the winner between the three types of automotive power was anybody's guess.

Riker, even though he pioneered in the development of electric vehicles, seemed to see the handwriting on the wall before it became legible to many other auto manufacturers. At any rate, he sold his electric automobile business for $2 million and joined a company that was then making steam automobiles and later switched over to gasoline engines.

There was a lot to be said in favor of electric automobiles. They ran quietly and smoothly, without the bone-shaking *chitty-chitty-bang-bang* vibrations and noxious fumes that were characteristic of the early gas buggies.

As the years passed, many different makes of electric automobiles became available—elegant, sedate, glass-enclosed vehicles, tiller-steered, and usually with a small vase for flowers in the upper front corner of the passenger compartment. They were especially beloved by gentle ladies who never aspired to belong to the brash young hot rod set that delighted in driving its noisy gas buggies at breakneck speeds.

The electric automobile's fatal shortcoming was the short distance it could be driven before its batteries had to be recharged. The last of them quietly whirred into oblivion in the early 1920s.

1901/ The Merry Oldsmobile

One of America's best-remembered automobile pioneers was a man by the name of Ransom E. Olds. He built his first car as far back as 1887. It was a steamer. During the next few years, other experimental models followed. But none of them were very successful.

Finally, in 1901, he designed and built a wonderful little gas buggy—this curved-dash runabout. He was convinced that this was the kind of automobile most Americans wanted. Just as his company, the Olds Motor Works, was getting ready to put the car into production, disaster struck.

One noon, when Mr. Olds and his workers had gone to lunch, the factory caught on fire. One employee, returning early, saw the clouds of smoke billowing from the building and dashed inside. Fortunately, the flames had not yet reached the pilot model of the gas buggy, which happened to be standing by the door. So he pushed it to safety, out into the street. Everything else was lost in the fire, including blueprints, patterns, and machine tools.

Although most of the building was gutted by flames, the foundry section remained standing. The workmen quickly cleared away the debris and made this part of the building their temporary workshop.

Their first job was to disassemble the prototype automobile they had rescued, down to the last nut and bolt. Then they made new drawings of each separate part and sent them out to various shops and factories in the Detroit area. Soon, newly built parts for the entire car began to flow back to them.

Olds was in business again.

This was probably the first example of what was later to become common practice in the automobile industry—farming out orders for parts to other manufacturers. Some of the men and companies who helped keep Olds in business later became well-known automobile manufacturers themselves, which is one of the reasons Detroit eventually became the Motor City of the U.S.A.

The car made automobile history in still another way. With a plentiful supply of identical parts coming in day after day, it became the first automobile that could be produced in quantity. More than 400 of them were built the first year, more than 2,000 in 1902, and almost 4,000 in 1903. It was America's first mass-produced automobile.

The rugged little vehicle had a wheelbase of only 67 inches and sat high on its springs, resembling a grasshopper at rest. The single-cylinder engine, with its big flywheel, delivered about 5hp and was tucked neatly out of sight, under the seat. Like most other cars of its time, it had a tiller for steering. Power was transmitted to the rear axle by a single chain drive. With its 2-speed transmission in top gear, it was able to tool down the road at a sprightly 20mph.

The Olds curved-dash runabout, priced at only $650, became so popular that a song was written about it, long before the days of radio and singing commercials. The name of the song was "In My Merry Oldsmobile."

1902/ *Thomas*

When young Edwin Ross Thomas of Buffalo, New York, built this automobile in 1902, he had a very special reason for making it such an elegant-looking car. It is said that he and his bride used the runabout for their wedding trip.

This first Thomas automobile was a fine car, with a sturdy 12hp 1-cylinder engine, a 2-speed transmission, and a chain-driven rear axle.

Note the resplendent carbide headlamp mounted over the underslung gill-tube radiator, and the pair of shiny brass oil lamps on each side of the dash. Having heard that a bicyclist, one night, had mistaken an approaching gas buggy for a pair of cyclists and had tried to ride *between* them, with dire results, Thomas painted a broad red stripe on one of his lamps and a green stripe on the other as a warning that this was a car, not two bicycles. The explosive *pop-pop* of the gas buggy's engine might have seemed warning enough, but Thomas was taking no chances—especially on his honeymoon trip.

Impressive as this handsome runabout was, the Thomas company's real claim to fame was an automobile it built five years later—the 4-cylinder, 60hp Thomas Flyer. This was the car that made American automobile history by winning the 22,000-mile race from New York, *westbound*, to Paris, in 1908. Six cars, 5 of them of foreign make, were entered in the race. They left Times Square, New York, on February 12, with 250,000 spectators cheering the start of the "impossible" race.

The first hazard was encountered not far from New York—a howling blizzard. Battering its way through deep snowdrifts, the Thomas was the first to arrive in Chicago, 13 days later. Then on to San Francisco, slogging through hub-deep mud, fording rivers, threading scorching desert trails and icy mountain passes.

By the time the Thomas Flyer reached Seattle, its only remaining threats were the German car, which had broken down in Utah and traveled the last 1,000 miles to Seattle by rail, and the Italian car. These two vehicles continued by ship to the Russian port of Vladivostok. But the Thomas, abiding by the official rules for the race, was shipped instead to Yokohama and was the first car ever to drive across Japan on its 350 miles of primitive narrow roads.

Crossing the barren Russian steppes, the three cars now left in the race were forced to drive for hundreds of miles over the wooden ties of the Trans-Siberian Railroad tracks, for many of the roads were impassable.

On July 30, the patched-up, travel-worn Thomas arrived in Paris and was declared the winner for having run 13,341 miles under its own power. Today, restored to almost the exact condition in which it won its historic 170-day race, the intrepid Thomas Flyer reposes as an exhibit in a Nevada automobile museum.

1903 / *Cadillac*

If you had plunked down $850 for this handsome new 1903 Cadillac, here are a couple of things you'd have to do, according to a little book entitled *Instructions for Drivers and Caretakers*.

To fill the radiator—those rows of disk-covered tubes at the front of the car—you would take out the leather-upholstered seat cushion and insert a funnel into a pipe leading to a water tank under the seat. When the tank was full, the water traveled to the radiator through a seamless copper tube and then flowed back to the engine.

Taking care of the car's chain drive was a more complicated matter. "About once a month," it says in the owner's manual, "the chain should be taken off the sprocket, soaked in gasoline, and cleaned with a stiff brush to remove grit and dirt. Then take four pounds of beef tallow, a pound of graphite, and one pint of heavy lubricating oil. Heat and stir. When thoroughly melted, dip the chain into the hot mixture, leaving it there long enough so that it soaks into all the small bearings. Then let the chain drip, wipe the outside, and replace on the sprocket."

Perhaps if you had been rich enough to buy the Cadillac in the first place, you would also have had a faithful "caretaker" to attend to messy jobs like this.

In those days, $850 was a lot of money, but the Cadillac was a lot of car, too. It had a 1-cylinder, 6½hp engine which was mounted horizontally, midway within the car's frame, with the cylinder toward the rear. It could be cranked from either side. There were 2 forward speeds and a reverse gear.

The car had no top or windshield, but it did have a steering wheel, a bulb horn attached to the steering column, and 3 handsome brass kerosene lamps, 2 at the front and 1 at the rear. Its dainty fenders were metal, and were attached to the wooden body by iron brackets.

Although the car came as a smart 2-passenger runabout, it could quickly be converted into a 4-passenger automobile by fastening a back seat, or tonneau, to the chassis. The entrance to the tonneau was through a small door at the rear.

Even the earliest Cadillacs were noted for their fine workmanship, a reputation that has lasted down to the present day. And it was the first to achieve standardization of parts through precision manufacturing. In 1908, to demonstrate this fact, the company shipped three of its cars to England for the Dewar Trophy Test, which was conducted by the Royal Automobile Club.

Upon arrival, the three cars were completely dismantled. All their various parts were thoroughly mixed and piled in a heap. The cars were then reassembled from the scrambled parts and were driven to a nearby track for a 500-mile run. All three completed the test with flying colors.

1904 / *Franklin*

When young "H.H." Franklin became old enough to strike out on his own, he left his boyhood farm home in upstate New York and got a job in a factory that built sleighs. Some years and hundreds of sleighs later, he decided to move on, even though his boss offered to make him a partner in the business if he would stay.

Giving up his job, he purchased a small-town newspaper. One day, happening to hear about a new manufacturing process called die cutting, he sold his newspaper, bought the patent for the process, and set up shop in Syracuse, where he started making small metal products.

In the spring of 1901, when "H.H." had become a well-known and prosperous manufacturer, he met an engineering graduate, just out of Cornell, by the name of John Wilkinson, who invited him to go for a ride in a new gas buggy he had built. Franklin was so impressed by the ride that he said he would put up the money Wilkinson needed to continue the development of his horseless carriage. By the end of 1902, the H.H. Franklin Manufacturing Company had built and sold 13 of the automobiles.

The early Franklins had something that set them apart from other automobiles: an *air-cooled* engine. As a matter of fact, every Franklin ever built, from the first model to the last Franklin to be produced, in 1934, was powered by an air-cooled engine.

The original 7hp Franklin engine had 4 cylinders, cast separately, with a series of 21 cooling fins on each cylinder jacket. The engine was positioned crosswise in the chassis, with its flywheel and detachable hand crank on the right. The drive-gear casing protruded from the left end of the crankshaft and propelled the car by a chain running to the rear axle.

The rugged 4-cylinder cars were dependable and amazingly trouble-free. Their "chicken-wire," "see-through" air scoops identified them immediately as cars that needed no radiator. Unlike the conventional water-cooled engine, the Franklin engine couldn't freeze up in zero weather or boil over on hot days. To convince skeptics of the engine's efficiency, a Franklin was driven one summer *in low gear* all the way from Walla Walla, Washington, to San Francisco. It arrived there cool as the proverbial cucumber.

In 1904, an air-cooled Franklin made a record-smashing cross-country trek from the West Coast to New York. Skimming over scorching desert trails, threading its way along dry, boulder-strewn riverbeds, chugging through sand up to its chain sprocket, fording streams, and scaring the wits out of gold prospectors and Indians, it completed its historic run in less than 33 days.

The Franklin was one of the finest automobiles ever produced in America, and continued to be, for more than three decades. Then came the depression, and the company folded.

1905 / *Buick*

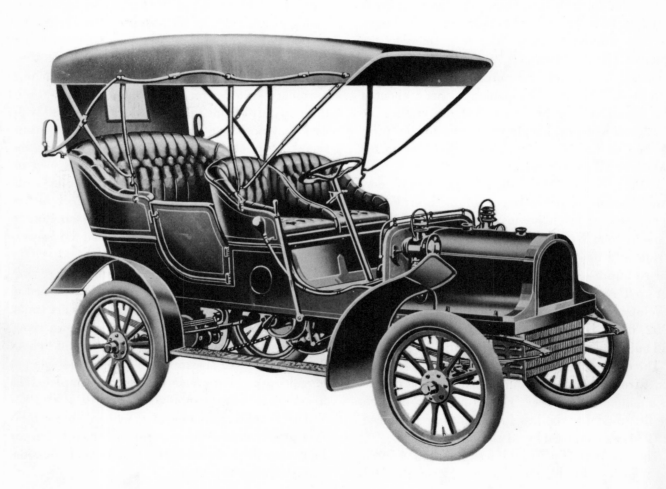

David D. Buick was a pioneer Detroit manufacturer of plumbing equipment. He was also an inventor. Among other things, he found a way to seal a thick layer of smooth porcelain to a rough cast-iron surface—and the world's first white bathtub was born.

Useful as this invention was, the name Buick was destined to become known to countless millions of people for quite another reason. In 1903 he designed and built a jaunty 2-cylinder horseless carriage. Naturally, he called it a Buick. Friends admired the car and asked him to build more of them. So he borrowed some money and formed the Buick Motor Company. He turned out 16 cars that year, and 21 more the following year.

Perhaps the most famous of the early Buicks was this grand old 1905 touring car. Known as the Model C, it was a very advanced car for its day. It not only had a number of engineering features that were brand-new, but its stylish 5-passenger body was something to behold. Priced at $1,200, total production for the year was 750 cars.

This automobile's horizontal 2-cylinder engine, with its mechanically operated overhead valves, was the forerunner of the valve-in-head motors that have powered Buick cars ever since. Mounted beneath the front seat, the dependable little "two-lunger" developed 22hp and propelled the vehicle by means of a planetary transmission—2 speeds forward and 1 reverse—with direct chain drive to the rear axle.

The car's fluted, oblong radiator was suspended from the chassis between the 2 front wheels. The storage space under the hood itself contained 2 tanks—one for water, the other for gasoline—with 2 filler caps protruding from the top of the hood.

The big wood-spoked wheels were equipped with 30-inch pneumatic tires mounted on clincher rims. The job of changing one of those early tires after a puncture, then patching the hole, pumping up the tire, and forcing it back on the rim again was enough to make many a pioneer automobile owner regret that he ever graduated from driving a horse and buggy.

Buicks were excellent automobiles right from the start, but their young manufacturer soon found that building and selling automobiles was much more complicated than turning out bathtubs. He ran into financial difficulties and decided to sell his business. In 1908, the Buick Motor Company became the cornerstone of the newly formed General Motors Corporation, where the name Buick and the car's reputation lived on to become one of the great success stories in American automobile history. It was an automobile that always tried to live up to its famous slogan: "When Better Cars Are Built, Buick Will Build Them."

1906/ Lozier

A lot of people say they have never even heard of the Lozier, but in the early 1900s it was well known as one of America's largest and best-built automobiles. At $4,500 and up, it was also one of the most expensive.

The Lozier father and son were manufacturers of bicycles in Ohio before the turn of the century. When the father retired, the son moved to Plattsburg, New York. There, on the shore of Lake Champlain, he established himself in business as a maker of marine gasoline engines for motorboats and launches.

Soon, however, he became more interested in wheels than propellers. First he built a tiller-steered steam buggy with wire wheels, patterned more or less after the earlier Stanley Steamer. Although history records it as being a good car, young Lozier gave up the idea of using steam and began to experiment with gasoline-engine automobiles, which were really more down his alley. The first Loziers were offered to the public in 1905 and 1906.

There was nothing flashy about the appearance of the Lozier. It was sedate and quietly elegant—a "proper" automobile for people of wealth and good taste to own. Its honeycomb radiator was broad-shouldered, and the hood was almost flat. Its well-honed 4-cylinder engine boasted a ball-bearing crankshaft, which was something of an engineering "first." With a 4-speed sliding gearbox and a beautiful $2\frac{1}{2}$ to 1 gear ratio in overdrive fourth, the Lozier could hum its double chains at a far-from-sedate speed of almost 70mph.

But Lozier engineers built more than speed into their car. Do you know what a sprag is? It's a short pole that wagon drivers used to attach to their rear axle by a hinge. If a driver wanted to stop and rest his horse, going up a steep hill, he would let the sprag drop down. Digging into the road, between the wheels, it braced the wagon and prevented it from rolling backward.

The Lozier car had a similar, very ingenious, device on the brake drum of its differential. The owner's manual called it a "dog-and-ratchet backstop"—a "dog" being a mechanical version of a sprag. The operator of a Lozier knew he could safely bring his car to a dead stop on a steep hill because the dog would instantly pop into the teeth of the ratchet and hold the car motionless, even without the use of the brake. A neat trick! (About forty years later, another manufacturer used it briefly on his cars, too.)

In 1912, the Lozier company moved to Detroit, where it continued to build about 1,200 cars a year. But even though it reduced its prices to lure more buyers, sales kept falling off. The company went out of business a few years later—which is why you, too, may never have heard of the great Lozier automobile.

1907/ *Peerless*

Packard, Peerless, and Pierce-Arrow—those were the three glorious "P's" of motordom after the turn of the century. The Peerless—big, luxurious, beautifully built, fast, and expensive—was to remain one of this illustrious trio of truly great motorcars for the next thirty years.

Like the Lozier and some other pioneer automobiles, the Peerless had bicycles in its family tree. Born in Cleveland, it was the product of a concern that had been making bikes (and clothes wringers) since 1869. With such an ancestry, it was only natural that the first Peerless horseless carriage would have a tubular frame and bicycle wheels.

It wasn't until a man by the name of Louis Mooers joined the company as chief engineer that the Peerless started to become a *big* automobile. Instead of single-cylinder gas buggies, 2-cylinder vehicles soon came rolling out of the factory. And as early as 1903, the company made news by proudly displaying its first 4-cylinder car. With its spacious 4-passenger tonneau body, it was just about the biggest and longest automobile at the Auto Show.

The company made headlines again in 1907 with its new 6-cylinder car, which became the pride and joy of wealthy motorists who had been waiting for a big, easy-handling, high-speed automobile like that.

Peerless-built automobiles had already gained a reputation for being able to move fast, largely because of the exploits of the special Green Dragon racer which Louis Mooers built for daredevil Barney Oldfield.

The Peerless Green Dragon was a monster-on-wheels. Its massive engine had barrellike pistons a full 6 inches in diameter. The fearless Barney, barnstorming his way across the country, smashed every circular-track record of the day in this car. Crowds at county fairs used to go wild with excitement as he roared past the stands, grimly hunched over the wheel, for they knew they were probably watching still another speed record being made. They were seldom disappointed. Oldfield once broke 12 records in 2 days. Some of them, it is true, were his own, but every time he was able to lop even a second or two from one of his previous records, spectators cheered until they were hoarse.

The Peerless company gradually dropped out of racing, devoting itself solely to building high-quality passenger cars, some of which cost $5,000 or more. The well-known Peerless slogan, "All That the Name Implies," said everything that needed to be said about this superbly crafted, highly respected automobile.

But in the early 1930s, just as the fine old company was preparing to bring out a luxury V-16 to meet its growing multicylinder competition, it fell victim to the depression. Its final masterpiece never went into production.

1908/ Model T Ford

FORD MOTOR COMPANY.

This was the year Henry Ford's big dream came true—a car with standardized parts, a car that could be built so cheaply that almost everybody could afford to own one. People made jokes about the awkward-looking Model T and called it the Tin Lizzie. But they loved it.

Under its hinged, angular hood was an amazingly simple water-cooled 4-cylinder engine that let it perk along at a brisk 40mph. Its planetary transmission, lined with friction bands, was operated by pedals. There were three of them. You pressed down the one on the left to put the car into low. When released, it flipped back and you were in high. The pedal in the middle was for reverse. The one on the far right was the brake.

How the Model T became the first automobile to be built on a moving assembly line is an interesting story. . . .

At first, it was put together the same way other manufacturers were building cars. The bare frame, or chassis, was left standing in one spot on the factory floor. While workmen attached the axles and wheels and installed the engine, helpers kept bringing additional parts, until the car was finally completed. It took about 12½ hours to assemble each automobile.

Then Henry Ford had an idea. He rigged up a windlass with a 250-foot length of rope. When the windlass turned, it dragged a line of 25 car frames along the floor. Parts were stockpiled at various "stations" along the way, within easy reach when they were needed. Workmen, walking along beside the moving chassis, installed the parts as the frames crept along.

This method worked fine, until, as parts were added to one car after another, the load became too heavy and the rope broke.

Then Henry Ford thought of building an endless, power-driven conveyor on which the frames could be set. It was wide enough so that the workmen could stand on both sides of it, beside the chassis, riding along the few feet necessary to do their special jobs. They would then drop back and add the same parts to the next chassis. This way, it took only 93 minutes to assemble a Model T.

Mr. Ford enthusiastically predicted that someday automobiles could be built on a moving assembly line at the rate of one a minute. Not even he could guess that the day was to come when new cars would roll off the end of the Ford assembly line almost like popcorn—not one each minute, but one every 10 seconds.

During the nineteen years of Model T production, more than 15 million of them were built and sold. Banging and rattling across the land in ever-increasing numbers, they changed the way people lived and even the land itself, as better roads were built to accommodate them. So, while Henry Ford did not invent the American automobile, as some people believe, he probably did more than any other person, with his wonderful Model T, to make America a "nation on wheels."

1909 / *Maxwell*

The Maxwell was a great little car. For only $550 you could become the proud owner of the jaunty Model A Runabout, equipped with what the catalog described as "long rakish fenders and running-boards, 2 oil side lights, 1 oil tail light, and 1 rubber bulb horn with flexible tube."

Its 2-cylinder engine, with the cylinders horizontally opposed, was rated at 10hp. The car had a wheelbase of 82 inches and a 2-speed transmission with reverse gear. It came painted a bright Speedster Red. The customer was given no choice of colors.

If you were a doctor, and willing to spend a little more money for a car, you could get the 20hp Model DR (for "doctor") which, according to the catalog, was "built especially for physicians desiring a more powerful car than our standard runabouts, well adapted for hilly country and sandy roads." This car boasted 3 forward speeds and its color was always a vivid "Maxwell Green—no other choice."

The Maxwell was a well-built automobile, but like most other cars, it was at its best when treated with loving care. Simply lubricating it was almost a full-time job. They used to say that you could tell a Maxwell owner by his bruised knuckles.

Since the muddy roads of those days had a way of clogging a car's underbody, the owner usually had to hose down his Maxwell just to find the places that had to be oiled. Next, he would take up the floor mat, lift the floorboards, and unscrew the top of the transmission casing to check the oil level. Crankcase oil had to be changed once a week and there were 6 major areas to be lubricated if squeaks were to be kept to a minimum.

Oiling the magneto of an early Maxwell was a tricky job, too. There were 2 hard-to-find pinholes on the top of the magneto, each of which was supposed to get 2 drops of oil—no more, no less. The owner who was careless enough to spill oil on the outside of the casing could count on winding up with a fouled magneto.

Every grease cup on a Maxwell—and there were a dozen or more—had to be kept full and given a turn of the screw top once a day. And each season there was the brain-staggering chore of removing the car's wheels and packing them with heavy grease. A sobering warning in the owner's instruction book reminded him that "it is a delicate matter to adjust the wheels properly once they have been removed."

In spite of the care required to keep it in tip-top running condition, the Maxwell was one of the most dependable cars of its time. It turned in a near-perfect record in every Glidden Tour it entered, and was the outright victor in two of them.

In 1924, the Maxwell company was taken over by Walter P. Chrysler. "The Good Maxwell," after receiving a slight bit of face-lifting, became the first car to bear the Chrysler name.

1910/ *Packard* 30

Before the new Model 30 went into full production, according to a story told in an old Packard report, the engineers commandeered the first 4 factory-built cars and sent them hither and yon, with experienced company test-drivers at the wheel, on a series of closely supervised workout tours.

Each car was given an endearing nickname, for the Packard employees who had helped build the cars were eager to keep track of their favorite's exploits on the daily scoreboard logged by the engineering department.

The original Model 30, known as Brave Billy Buster, won cheers by making a record-breaking 706-mile run from Detroit to Chicago and return, while the Proud Runabout Tige, not to be outdone, dashed off to New York. In the meantime, Valiant Gasoline Gus headed west, rumbling over desert trails and mountain passes. Modest Number Four, with its less glamorous name, kept plugging steadily along, day and night, over miles of roads in the countryside surrounding Detroit.

Altogether, the 4 test cars demonstrated their stamina by clocking a total of more than 50,000 trouble-free miles—a considerable feat of derring-do in the days when automobiles were seldom used for long-distance travel except by the most adventuresome.

Following this impressive and well-publicized launching ceremony, the car went into production to become one of the most famous and best-loved of all Packards.

The Model 30 got its name from its efficient engine—a 4-cylinder power plant with a 5-inch bore and $5\frac{1}{2}$-inch stroke—which was advertised as delivering 30hp. Actually, its brake horsepower rating was closer to 85, but the Packard company was noted for keeping its claims on the conservative side.

The car cost a lot of money—$4,200 for the touring model and up to $5,500 for the stately limousine. It could also be had with a special close-coupled body, like this one, in which the rear seats were positioned ahead of the rear axle. Since the car had a very long wheelbase, this feature provided an exceptionally smooth ride for back-seat passengers.

Many people who could afford to own a luxurious Packard also kept a uniformed chauffeur. But knowing that there might be times when the master himself would wish to take over the wheel, the company equipped some of its models with a rumble seat in which the family chauffeur could sit when he was not doing the driving.

During the six years the Packard 30 remained in production, about 10,000 of them were built. By this time, the famous Packard slogan, "Ask the Man Who Owns One," was practically a byword throughout the land. The company felt that no other recommendation was needed for a car as great as a Packard.

1911 / *Chevrolet*

Some people are surprised when they learn that there actually was an automobile man named Mr. Chevrolet. There really were two of them. Both were well-known French racing drivers, although Louis Chevrolet gained more fame on American tracks than his brother Arthur.

One day in 1909, in need of a job, they went to Flint, Michigan, to see William C. Durant, who was then general manager of the Buick company. Durant, an automotive genius known as the "boy wonder" of Flint, staged an impromptu dirt-track race to see how well the brothers could handle his cars. Louis won the race, but both of them were hired as members of the official Buick racing team.

Louis Chevrolet happened to be an engineer as well as a racing driver. He had long dreamed of designing and building an automobile that would be suitable for America's rapidly improving roads. He showed some of his experimental designs to Durant, who was impressed. He encouraged Louis to continue his experiments.

Not long afterward, Durant left Buick to organize a company of his own. He took his friend Chevrolet with him to carry on the development of the new car.

The 1911 experimental model—Louis Chevrolet himself at the wheel—was the first automobile he built. It was a large 5-passenger touring car with a 120-inch wheelbase—longer, by 1 inch, than today's most deluxe Chevy sedan. Under its hood was a 6-cylinder engine with a displacement of 229 cubic inches, which was a lot of engine for those days.

Louis Chevrolet built 4 more experimental cars. The fifth version got the final vote as an automobile worthy of bearing the name of Durant's newly formed Chevrolet Motor Company of Michigan. They called it the Classic Six and put it into production. By the end of the year, 2,999 Classic Six models had rolled off the line and found their way to eager customers. The car was priced at $2,150, "f.o.b. Detroit," which was a considerable sum of money.

It was a good first-year record for the company, but not good enough. Durant realized that if he ever hoped to catch up with Henry Ford's fast-selling Tin Lizzie, he would have to offer the public a lighter, less expensive automobile. The 2 cars that followed the Classic Six looked as if they might turn the trick. First came the famous Royal Mail roadster, in 1914. This was followed by the popular Baby Grand Chevrolet. Both cars had 4-cylinder engines and were priced at only $750 (not including the spare tire, which cost extra).

By the end of 1918, when the company had become a division of General Motors, it was turning out Chevrolets at the rate of 150,000 a year. It still had a long distance to go to overtake the Tin Lizzie, but Chevrolet was on its way.

1912 / *Simplex*

They didn't call it a sports car in those days, for the term hadn't yet been invented. It was simply a "sporty" car.

The Simplex was a tough breed, with racing in its veins—one of the fastest and most powerful automobiles of its time. It was an especially eager contestant in the grueling 24-hour dirt-road grinds that were so popular with the wealthy young sporting set in the early 1900s. So eager, in fact, that it usually won, sometimes streaking across the finish line 50 miles ahead of its nearest competitor.

If you wanted to compete in a Vanderbilt Cup race—or just bowl along the avenue in a car everyone would turn around to look at—the Simplex was for you. Its bare chassis cost $4,500. You paid extra for its custom-built speedster body.

What you got for your money was this: frame, drive shafts, and axles built of Krupp chrome-nickel steel from Germany; a 40-gallon gas tank (the car gulped fuel, and gas pumps were few and far between); a smaller tank, mounted ahead of the gas tank, containing 13 gallons of oil to be pressure-fed to the engine (both tanks had quick-opening, racing-type filler caps); three spare tires, strapped to the rear of the car; a 4-speed gate-slot gearshift; and a handcrafted 4-cylinder T-head engine, cylinders cast in pairs, with 2 spark plugs in each cylinder.

It was a brute of a car. Although the Simplex people modestly rated the engine at 50hp, its actual output was considerably more than that. The car could sustain a speed of 80mph almost effortlessly. Having a bore and stroke of 5¾ inches, the engine's 4 big pistons would be pumping at a leisurely 1800rpm even when the car was nudging 90mph. (The high-speed engines of modern cars, with their smaller pistons and shorter strokes, usually turn up 4000rpm to attain this speed.)

The 1912 Simplex, with its long 128-inch wheelbase, was one of the few cars that still had right-hand drive and one of the last of the chain-driven automobiles.

Because of the car's double chain drive linkup, there was a neat trick Simplex owners could fall back on whenever they wanted to take the trouble to do it. By simply changing the size of the 2 removable front chain sprockets, they could change the gear ratio of the car. For driving around town, 23-tooth sprockets gave the best gear ratio. For faster driving, in open country, 25-tooth sprockets were the thing, while 27-tooth sprockets, according to old-timers, were strictly for daredevils, speed demons, and fools.

Production of the Simplex car ended upon America's entry into World War I, when the company converted its plant to build V-8 Hispano-Suiza aircraft engines.

1913/ *Mercer Raceabout*

One day not long ago, several thousand eager old-car buffs gathered in Brookline, Massachusetts, where 65 antique and classic automobiles were about to be auctioned off to the highest bidders.

Bidding was spirited right from the start. The first 10 cars were quickly sold. Then, at a signal from the auctioneer, the owner of a bright yellow 1913 Mercer Raceabout drove his beautifully restored car into the auction tent. He and his car were greeted by a round of applause. The bidding started, went to $25,000, then to $35,000. When a bid of $40,000 was heard, the owner jubilantly gunned his engine. As the deep-throated 58hp rumble filled the tent, there came a final bid, for $45,000.

When the proud new owner took possession of the car, a disappointed bidder was heard to remark, "Ten years ago I could have bought one for ten thousand dollars, but I couldn't make up my mind to spend that much money for a forty-five-year-old car. I could kick myself when I think of it," he added.

The glamorous Mercer Raceabout, when new, had cost about $2,200. That may not seem like a fortune when compared with the price of one of today's cars, but it was then, when a new Model T Ford could be had for only $550.

With the possible exception of the Stutz Bearcat, the low-slung Mercer was the most exciting and most coveted sports car of its time. Sleek, fast, and flashy, its stripped-down body consisted simply of 2 bucket seats, floorboards and instrument panel, a circular "monocle" windshield clamped to the steering post to afford some measure of protection to the driver (but none to his passenger), and 2 spare tires mounted at a jaunty angle in back of the gas tank. The occupants of the car could count on a thrilling and rather breezy ride when the Raceabout hit its top speed of between 75 and 80mph.

The 4-cylinder, T-head engine compartment was covered with a plain "doghouse" hood, held securely in place by a sporty leather strap. The car had an outboard hand-brake lever and 3-speed "gate" gearshift, together with a rubber-bulb brass horn and an acetylene cylinder of gas for its large drum headlamps. The 4 big wheels, fully exposed beneath rakish fenders, told at a glance that here was a car capable of rolling back the miles at a lively clip on the open road. And it was. The Mercer always gave a good account of itself in the races it entered.

The famous Mercer Raceabout was introduced in 1911 and continued in production through 1914. Altogether, only about 500 of them were ever built. Only a dozen or so still exist. If you can find one for $10,000, it's a bargain!

1914/ *Stutz Bearcat*

Back in the days when "Twenty-three, skidoo!" was a real groovy slang expression, the Stutz Bearcat and the Mercer Raceabout were rivals for the unofficial title of King of the Road.

Owners of the two cars felt very strongly that *theirs* was the better car. Mercer fans would call out, "You must be nuts to drive a Stutz." This corny quip would invariably evoke an equally snappy retort: "There's nothing worser than a Mercer." Actually, these two sporty runabouts had a lot in common. Both were great cars.

When the first Stutz was built, its designer, Harry Stutz, quietly entered it in the 1911 Indianapolis 500 Sweepstakes at the last moment. Although the surprise entry finished in 11th place, its performance was so impressive that it became known overnight as "the car that made good in a day." Two years later, a Stutz copped 3rd place in the legendary 500 and went on to win the United States road-racing championship.

The most famous of all Stutz models, the Bearcat, came out in 1913. Painted a fire-engine red, bright blue, or canary yellow, its 4-cylinder T-head engine revved up a hefty 60hp. Slightly more powerful than the Mercer, the car had a top speed of close to 85mph.

Like the Mercer, the body of the Stutz Bearcat was stripped down to its bare essentials: front and rear fenders over large wheels, a pair of leather-upholstered bucket seats, a squared-off trunk behind the gas tank, and a spare tire. It, too, had an outside 3-speed gearshift and brake lever within easy reach of the driver's right hand. At idling speed, the rhythmic *boom, boom, boom* of its barrellike pistons was music to the ear.

The Stutz Bearcat remained in production until about 1920. Even though that was the year the last one rolled off the line, it is somehow still tagged by oldsters as a spirited symbol of the Roaring Twenties and the long-gone era of "flappers" and "flaming youth." They associate it in their minds with Hollywood stars of the silent films who owned one, and carefree, well-heeled youths in raccoon coats.

In the early 1930s, an attempt was made to revive this car and everything it stood for among lovers of spectacular cars. The Stutz Company called the new one the Super Bearcat. Powered by an 8-cylinder, 156hp engine, it was factory-guaranteed to do 100mph. But the new car didn't grab the heart and bring a gleam to the eye the way its famous forerunner did. It was not a success. In 1936, the company folded.

The old Stutz Bearcat was a very special breed of car. Its name, and the car itself, belonged to the era that made it famous.

1915/ *Packard Twin Six*

The Packard Twin Six was a truly great automobile. It was powered by America's first 12-cylinder engine—the brainchild of Jesse Vincent, who had become Packard's chief engineer in 1910.

When the car was introduced, in 1915, people thronged by the thousands into Packard showrooms across the country to see it. The price of the touring model was $2,750. The elegant limousine cost $4,150. The Twin Six was definitely a luxury car. To own one was a mark of distinction.

In Oklahoma, when oil was discovered on land belonging to the Osage Indians, it was considered quite the thing for a chief to spend a portion of his unexpected fortune for a Packard Twin Six. One brave, who was obviously more at home on a bareback Indian pony than behind the wheel of an automobile, paid $7,000 for a custom-built version of the car. An hour later, he telephoned from a nearby desert town saying that he had smashed his car and wanted another one just like it. Still another oil-rich Osage chief almost missed out. When he arrived at the Packard showroom in Tulsa, he found that the dealer had just sold his last Twin Six passenger car. The only model remaining was a resplendent white Packard hearse. The chief bought it and drove off happily with his family squatting inside it.

The luxurious Packard Twin Six was beloved by royalty, too. Czar Nicholas II of Russia drove one. So did his brother, Grand Duke Michael. Quite a few of the cars were bought by wealthy Indian rajahs. One such potentate ordered 3 of them, all fitted with costly custom-built bodies.

In spite of its size and weight, the Packard Twin Six was an unusually responsive automobile. The secret of the engine's smooth-as-silk performance was its 2 opposed banks of small jeweled pistons, each measuring a scant 3 inches in diameter with a 5-inch stroke. When you slipped the car into gear, it moved off silently, with an eager, whispering surge of power. One of the impressive things about this Packard was that it could be throttled down almost to idling speed in high gear and continue to roll along at a steady 3mph. Then, still in high, it could be accelerated to normal road speed in a matter of seconds, and would soon be pushing the needle up to the 80mph mark, which in those days was pretty close to flying.

Shortly after the launching of the standard 85hp Twin Six, Vincent built a special high-compression version of the engine, with which Ralph de Palma, the famous racing driver, broke many a track record. Later, when Vincent was asked to develop a new aircraft engine for the Army Air Corps, he based its design on that of his original Twin Six. The result was the famed Liberty Engine of World War I.

The last car in the great Packard Twin Six series was produced in 1923, although a few custom-built V-12s were manufactured on special order as late as 1939.

1916/ *Hudson Super Six*

Roy D. Chapin is best remembered in automobile history as the young Oldsmobile employee who made headlines in 1901 by driving one of the little curved-dash runabouts from Detroit to New York in 7½ days. He delivered the mud-spattered gas buggy just in time to have it washed and entered in the Auto Show at Madison Square Garden.

But Chapin's real claim to fame is the fact that he later became the builder of one of America's finest and most popular automobiles. Instead of giving the car his own name, as most early auto makers did, he called it the Hudson, after the Detroit department store magnate who had put up most of the money for the venture.

The first Hudson—the rugged 22hp Model 20 Roadster—rolled out of the factory on July 3, 1909. Priced at only $900, it was an immediate success. By the end of the year, more than 4,000 of them had been built and sold—a new first-year record in the industry.

Hudsons became renowned as well-engineered cars with plenty of speed. The Mile-a-Minute Roadster, built in 1913, was guaranteed to do 60mph, which was a frisky clip back in those days.

The really big news came in 1916, with the introduction of a beautiful new automobile known as the Hudson Super Six, the first American car to have a high-compression cylinder head. The 76hp, 6-cylinder engine, with its unheard-of 5 to 1 compression ratio, was hailed as a landmark in engine design.

Ralph Mulford, the well-known racing driver, found the new Super Six very much to his liking. He took one and rammed it over the Daytona sands at 102mph to set a new 1-mile record. Then, on the Sheepshead Bay dirt track, he set a new 24-hour record with an average speed of 74.8mph. Aided by the publicity resulting from these two record-breaking runs, sales of the Super Six totaled 10,000 cars in the first six months.

The keen styling of the Hudson Super Six made it well-liked, too. We can only imagine that this particular model, with its special, elegant, air-scoop brougham top, was meant to be driven at a sedate speed about town, and not on the dirt track.

The Hudson company gathered still more laurels for its wonderful Super Six by staging America's first *round-trip* transcontinental run. A standard touring car was driven from San Francisco to New York in 5 days, 3 hours, and 31 minutes. Pausing only long enough to turn around, it then tore back to San Francisco in 5 days, 17 hours, and 32 minutes.

Although the company dropped the Super Six designation on its cars in 1917, the Hudson automobile was destined to enjoy public favor for another four decades.

1917/ *Saxon*

Mrs. Alice Snitzer Burke, here at the wheel of her Saxon roadster, was a suffragette. So was her companion, Miss Neil Richardson. Their battle cry was, "Votes for women!" If American men could go to the polls and vote, they asked, why couldn't women, too? They said it was time to change all that sort of nonsense.

So they took the first step toward spreading the message by buying this spanking-new Saxon automobile, for $395. They had to pay $70 extra to get electric lights and a starter. Then they set out to tour the country. For five months they drove over the highways and byways of the United States, from coast to coast, covering a total distance of 10,000 miles, waving their Votes-for-Women banner and encouraging the faint of heart to carry on the good fight.

Their decision to buy a Saxon had been a wise one. It didn't cost very much, and besides, its manufacturer said that it would travel 28 to 36 miles on a gallon of gasoline, 75 to 100 miles per pint of oil, and up to 5,000 miles on a set of tires.

Even lady drivers found the Saxon an easy car to park, for its chassis had a wheelbase of only 96 inches. Its power plant was a light, high-speed 4-cylinder engine of 18hp, which was more than ample to move the pert little vehicle along at a lively clip, especially on the level.

The first Saxons, introduced in 1914, had a 2-speed rear-axle gearbox and wire wheels. They were more like cyclecars than conventional automobiles. Then came wooden wheels and a 3-speed gearbox. The small 2-seater was now a real automobile.

The Saxon Motor Car Company claimed that the car contained 9 major parts found only in automobiles costing as much as $4,800. As an example, it cited the Saxon radiator, which was made by the same company that built radiators for the Pierce-Arrow. It was a very light car, but according to an early Saxon advertisement, it offered "fullest riding comfort through the use of specially designed vanadium springs, which no less than 15 higher priced cars have already adopted."

The keen little car caught the public fancy. In its peak year, 27,800 of them were built and delivered. In 1922, the Saxon company tried briefly and unsuccessfully to invade the 6-cylinder market, then gave up, going back to its original 4-cylinder car. But the demand for such a car had faded. Convinced that the day of the American "minicar" was over, the company stopped building them and went out of business.

Two years earlier, American women had won the right to vote. It's nice to think that perhaps the two gritty ladies in their cross-country Saxon helped to turn the trick.

1918/ *Owen Magnetic*

They called it "the car with a thousand speeds." Although it was powered by a conventional 6-cylinder engine, the Owen Magnetic was an oddity because of one thing: its transmission was patterned after the gearless magnetic transmission that turned the drive shaft and propellers of the U.S. battleship *New Mexico*. Introduced in 1914, the luxurious Owen Magnetic excited great public interest and was driven by thousands of loyal owners during the seven years it was produced.

The car was the brainchild of Ray M. Owen, who had formerly been an engineer with a firm that built electric automobiles in Cleveland, Ohio. It had no clutch pedal and no gears to shift. The driver put his car into its many different speed ranges, from start to high, simply by gradually advancing a little gadget that slid along a notched quadrant on the steering wheel.

One enthusiastic owner, after driving his new Owen Magnetic, wrote: "The starting, increasing, and diminishing its speed is so smooth and free of sudden jars, jerking and jumping, that the movement of the car suggests a yacht leaving its mooring, always floating along."

The company itself, in an early catalog, described the virtues of its car by saying, "It combines the power and efficiency of the gasoline engine, the flexibility of the steam engine, and the smoothness of an electric dynamo. Every operation, from the starting of the car, to a veritable crawl, and so on

up to a speed of 60 miles per hour, is controlled by a single, simple little lever attached to the steering wheel."

So now let's find out, in terms that are not too technical, how these wonders were accomplished. To begin with, there was no direct mechanical connection between the Owen Magnetic's engine and the rear wheels of the car. Instead of a flywheel, a generator and a horseshoe-shaped electric magnet were attached to the rear end of the engine's crankshaft. On the forward end of the car's drive shaft was an electric motor whose armature fitted into the air space inside the whirling magnet. Electric current, transmitted from the engine's generator and magnet to the armature of the electric motor, provided the energy that turned the drive shaft and propelled the rear wheels. As simple as ABC.

Perhaps Mr. Owen's wonderful idea of applying the principle of a battleship's electric dynamo to an automobile was too advanced for its time, and caused garage mechanics too many headaches—although, in the 1950s, we were to find another auto maker trying to adapt a jet plane's gas turbine for use in his cars.

Automobile history is filled with the stories of men who dared to experiment with the seemingly impossible, constantly seeking to improve the efficiency of the great American motorcar. Some succeeded.

1919/ *Dodge*

The small-town Michigan brothers John and Horace Dodge got their start in business as bicycle makers, in 1899. A couple of years later, they moved to Detroit and set up a shop for the manufacture of automobile axles, transmissions, steering gears, and engine parts. Soon, thanks to big orders from Ford, Olds, and other pioneer auto makers, they had become the largest suppliers of automobile parts in the U.S.

In 1910, the brothers began laying plans to bring out a complete automobile under their own name. Four years later, as word spread that the Dodge car was about to appear, thousands of applications poured in from firms and individuals all over the country who wanted to get in on the ground floor as Dodge dealers. And people started sending in orders for the car, sight unseen.

On a blustery day in November, 1914, John and Horace Dodge unveiled their eagerly awaited automobile—a rugged 4-cylinder touring car they nicknamed Old Betsy. The Dodge Brothers factory, now teeming with 482 employees, swung into production. By the end of the year, 249 Dodge automobiles had rolled off the assembly lines.

The public's response to the new car was overwhelming. Priced at only $785, the Dodge soon gained worldwide renown as the most dependable car money could buy. In fact, it was because of the Dodge that a new word was coined and eventually found its way into the dictionary. The word: *dependability*.

By 1919, the Dodge brothers had 18,000 employees and their new, enlarged plant was turning out cars at the rate of 300 a day. The company was firmly established as a leader in the industry.

The most popular Dodge car of that year was a smart-looking all-steel sedan—America's first 4-door closed car. Powered by a standard 35hp 4-cylinder Dodge engine, the car came painted a handsome blue-black, with yellow wire wheels.

There were two things about the sedan that set it apart from other automobiles. Like all Dodges, its gearshift was "backwards." The sequence from low to high, and the reverse slot, was just the opposite from that in common use. And it had a silent starter, consisting of an oversized, 12-volt combined generator-and-starter. When the driver flipped a dash switch, the battery current flowed quietly to the motor generator and all of a sudden the engine would start. The whirring and grinding of starter gears was never heard by the owner of a Dodge.

In 1923, the millionth Dodge came off the assembly lines, but John and Horace Dodge were not there to witness the event. Inseparable during their lifetime, the two brothers died quite suddenly in 1920, within a few months of each other, after a brief illness. They were only in their fifties. The company was later bought by Walter Chrysler for the staggering sum of $175 million. Starting in 1928, it became the Dodge Division of the Chrysler Corporation.

1920/ Duesenberg Model A

The history of horsepower and speed contains few names that shine more brightly than Duesenberg, even though the first car to bear the name—the fabulous A—did not appear until 1920.

Actually, Fred and Augie Duesenberg embarked on their auto-making career back in 1904, when they opened up a garage in Des Moines, Iowa. It was there that they put together a spirited little 2-cylinder automobile they named the Mason, after the friend who had advanced them the money to set up their shop. The car was a demon of a hill-climber and as a dirt-track racer it took nobody's dust.

As time went on, the brothers began to specialize more and more in designing and building racing cars and high-speed engines, including a 12-cylinder marine engine with an output of 200hp. A speedboat in which two of these huge engines were installed, in tandem fashion, was the first to break the mile-a-minute speed record on water.

Years passed. The First World War found the Duesenbergs in a new plant of their own in New Jersey, turning out a steady stream of precision-built marine engines for navy subchasers, mammoth V-12 and V-16 aircraft engines, and sturdy 160hp, 4-cylinder tractor engines.

When the war ended, the two wizards of horsepower were free to return to their first love, racing cars. And to their dream of producing an elegant, wickedly expensive, passenger car. They sold their big New Jersey plant and moved to Indianapolis, where they formed the Duesenberg Automobile & Motor Company.

In early 1920, they built 3 prototype straight-8 engines, chassis-mounted them, and entered them in the Indianapolis Memorial Day 500. The cars came in 3rd, 4th, and 6th, and went on to set speed records at Daytona and other tracks all that season.

The company's crowning achievement came later that year when it proudly introduced its secretly-built first Duesenberg passenger car—the first American production automobile to have a straight-8 engine and 4-wheel hydraulic brakes. With its long, low, beautiful custom body, there was no mistaking the car's racing heritage, in appearance as well as performance.

To demonstrate the staying power of its race-proven straight-8 engine, a stock Duesenberg A made a simulated nonstop coast-to-coast run of 3,155 miles on the Indy Speedway. The only stops were at the pits, for tire changes, and even *then* the engine was kept running at a tach speed equivalent to 30mph. At times during its run, the mighty A hit speeds of well over 100mph. Its average for the grueling distance was better than 62mph—a record that was to stand for the next ten years.

The "Duzy A" was produced for about five years, virtually unchanged. After all, there was no reason to make changes in a car that already was considered to be as close to perfection as a car could be.

1921/ *Kissel Speedster*

Louis Kissel and his four sons had no idea of becoming automobile manufacturers when they set up a shop for making farm implements in Hartford, Wisconsin, back in the early 1900s.

But fate decreed otherwise. It all started when they hired a shop foreman who turned out to have unexpected talents. In his spare time, he kept tinkering with gasoline engines. They fascinated him. Then, one day, he surprised the Kissels by demonstrating an engine he had built himself.

Louis and his sons were quite excited about the engine and its possibilities. Obviously, what they needed now was an automobile to put it in. So they built a chassis and engaged a local sleigh builder to make a body for it. A rather odd-looking vehicle it was—something like a cutter on wheels. But it ran.

The Kissels, forgetting about farm implements as a business, built several more automobiles, improving them as they went along. In 1908, encouraged by their success, they formed the Kissel Motor Car Company. It wasn't long before they became well known as builders of sturdy touring cars, roadsters, and enclosed limousines. They called their early machines Kissel Kars. Either because of that klassy name, or in spite of it, the automobiles sold well and became very popular.

As the years passed, the company grew and prospered. But it always remained a relatively small family operation, with no more than 1,000 employees, most of whom were skilled craftsmen. Unlike the big Detroit auto companies, there were no mechanized assembly lines in the Kissel plant. Each car was built and put together by hand.

Perhaps the company's biggest stroke of luck was in hiring a coachbuilder named J. Frederick Werner. Before coming to America, Werner had been with the old Opel works in Germany, where he designed a number of special cars for the kaiser. His skill as a designer soon became apparent in the handsome new look of Kissel-built cars.

The most glamorous of them all were the keen Kissel Speedsters that made their appearance following the end of World War I and during the early 1920s. The low, smart, 2-passenger roadsters had wire wheels, a distinctive long, high cowl, rounded hood and radiator shell, and sporty curved fenders. They were beautiful little cars.

One of the best-known models was the Kissel Gold Bug Speedster, so-called because its standard color was chrome yellow. Today's collectors prize the Gold Bug highly, whenever they are lucky enough to find one.

The Kissel company never became a giant in the industry, for it did not go in for volume production. During its peak year, it built only about 3,000 cars. Then came the depression years, when cars that were more or less custom-built by old-time methods became too costly to buy. Kissel bowed out of the picture in 1931.

1922/ *Essex Coach*

The boxy Essex Coach was so square and ugly it was almost handsome, if such a thing is possible. Compared with today's low, sleek sedans, it was rather a funny-looking car. But then, the clothes people wore back in 1922 looked sort of funny, too, as you can see.

Although it was about as graceful as a packing crate on wheels, there was a very good reason for the square, angular appearance of the Essex Coach. A body like that could be factory-built in large numbers at a much lower cost than a body with pretty curves. For in those days, huge stamping presses for shaping sheet-metal body panels were still unknown. Each automobile body had to be built and machined by hand. Coachbuilders had to be almost as skilled as cabinetmakers. That was why, until the Essex came along, closed cars usually cost $500 to $1,000 more than open touring cars.

The mass-produced Essex Coach was a Hudson-built car. It was the brainchild of Roy D. Chapin, then president of the combined companies, who was convinced that a well-built closed automobile body, no matter how plainly styled, would appeal to thousands of people if it were priced low enough.

He was right. When the honest-looking coach went on display in dealer showrooms, the public made the happy discovery that it could now ride in closed-car comfort for only about $100 more than the cost of an open touring car. The Essex Coach,

priced at slightly over a thousand dollars, sold like hot cakes. During that first year, more than 30,000 of them rolled out of the factory and into the hands of eager customers.

The perky black car was a bargain any way you looked at it. Under its hood was an L-head 4-cylinder engine that delivered a whirlwind of power. The car became famed for its jackrabbit getaway at traffic lights, and for its lively acceleration on the open road.

In 1924, the four was replaced by a 6-cylinder engine and the price of the car was reduced to an even $1,000. The combination—more power at a lower price—boosted the car's popularity to new heights. That year, the company produced 74,523 of them. There was no doubt by then but that Roy Chapin's closed-car gamble had paid off well. The Essex Coach was one of the fastest-selling cars on the market.

All good things, especially in the ever-changing auto industry, come to an end. In 1933, after 3,-371,107 Essex cars had been produced, the car took on airs and changed its name to Essex Terraplane. A year or so later, Essex was dropped from the name altogether and the car called the Terraplane rolled along on its not-so-merry way.

But the career of the 4-square Essex Coach will always be remembered as one of the success stories of its era.

1923 / *Pierce-Arrow*

The birth of the aristocratic Pierce-Arrow, like that of many other American automobiles, took place under rather humble circumstances. George Norman Pierce, who fathered the marque, was actually a manufacturer of birdcages and iceboxes, in Buffalo, New York. Later, he added bicycles to his company's line of products.

In early 1900, when the snort of the sputtering horseless carriage began to be heard across the land, Pierce and his partners decided it would be a good idea to expand their thriving business by building automobiles.

With two of the gas buggies they designed in 1901, they made an astonishing reliability run to New York City. It was the first of many triumphant performances in which the early Pierce cars, and later, the company's Great Arrows, demonstrated to the public how well made they were. In 1909, when the names Pierce and Arrow had become almost household words, they were coupled together to form the company's new name: the Pierce-Arrow Motor Car Company. From that date, all its cars were known as Pierce-Arrows.

Classic-car buffs will probably argue from now until doomsday about which of all the American cars ever built was the finest. But few will dispute the fact that for craftsmanship and sheer elegance, the Pierce-Arrow of the teens and early 1920s was in a class by itself.

This beautiful phaeton is an excellent example of the car as it looked in that era. Like all Pierce-Arrows, it had unique fender-mounted headlamps, an idea first developed in 1912 by company designer Herbert Dawley and retained from then on.

Since Pierce-Arrows were luxury cars, designed for the wealthy "carriage trade," no detail was too small, no effort too great, to achieve the company's goal of perfection. At a time when it was customary for car manufacturers to drop a completed engine into a chassis after a brief "run-in" block test, Pierce-Arrow engineers became a legend in the industry for their painstaking workmanship.

To begin with, every engine was given a dynamometer test for a specific period of time. Even if it ran perfectly, it was then stripped down and every part was carefully checked. Reassembled, it was run again on the dynamometer in a special Silent Room, for the engineers "had a thing" about the *quietness* of the power plants they built. After another power-output test, the engine was given a road test in a bare chassis and then still another dynamometer test. Finally the body was installed and the completed car was road-tested again before shipment to the dealer.

During Prohibition, offshore rumrunners often converted Pierce-Arrow engines for use in their speedboats, not so much for their tremendous horsepower as their quietness—an unsought but sincere compliment from an unlikely source to the old-school craftsmen who strove so diligently to make their beloved Pierce-Arrow engines and motorcars "the finest in the world."

1924/ *Chrysler*

At the age of seventeen, Walter P. Chrysler was earning 7½ cents an hour as an engine-wiper in the Union Pacific Railroad shops. The Kansas-born lad came by his love for locomotives naturally, for he was the son of a railroad engineer. By the time he was thirty-two, he had worked his way up to a well-paid job as superintendent of the Chicago Great Western Railroad shops. Then he lost his heart all over again—to another kind of machinery on wheels.

It happened at the opening of the 1908 automobile show in Chicago. Young Chrysler had never owned a car. In fact, he didn't know very much about them. At the exhibition, he stood spellbound at the sight of a gleaming white Locomobile with red trim and a price tag of $5,000. The beautiful car fascinated him. Finally, knowing that his total cash amounted to about $700, he turned sadly away. But the next day he was back again. Unable to give up the idea of owning the car, he had sought out a banker friend and borrowed the staggering sum of $4,300 to cover the balance. The Locomobile was his.

For the next three months, Chrysler spent most of his time in his garage finding out what made an automobile tick. He completely disassembled it and studied the parts as they lay on the floor. Then he reassembled them, checking and rechecking them with his keen machinist's mind. He learned the inner workings of his Locomobile as thoroughly as he had known his beloved locomotives. And in

doing so, he became, once and for all, an automobile man.

The rest of the Chrysler success story is history: how he became works manager of the Buick factory, then president of the company; how he took on the job of putting the ailing Willys-Overland company on its feet again, and was then called in by the worried officers of the Maxwell company to help reorganize their firm. He ended up by buying the company and changing the Maxwell car into a car named Chrysler, and the company itself into a corporation bearing his own name.

The first Chrysler car, introduced in January, 1924, was actually the work of a team of engineers the boss called his "three musketeers"—a trio named Zeder, Skelton, and Breer. The heart of the car they designed was a smooth high-compression 6-cylinder engine that developed 68hp at 3,200rpm, giving the car a top speed of over 70mph. Low and well-styled, with a distinctive winged ornament on its radiator cap, it was the first volume-production automobile to have 4-wheel hydraulic brakes. Priced as low as $1,395, the car was an instant success. By the end of the first year more than 32,000 of them had been sold. Walter P. Chrysler had done it again.

Although the colorful auto magnate died in 1940, at the age of 65, he lived long enough to see his company become a billion-dollar corporation and one of Detroit's legendary Big Three, which it still is.

1925 / Jordan Playboy

Like the Mercer Raceabout and Stutz Bearcat of an earlier era, this handsome roadster was one of the most exciting cars of its day.

It was the creation of a Cleveland auto maker by the name of Edward S. ("Ned") Jordan. Many years later, talking about the car with friends, he admitted it had been inspired by a swanky Packard roadster he happened to see one day in a New York custom-body showroom. Hastily sketching the outline of the $10,000 dreamboat on the back of an envelope, he took it back to his own shop to give his designers an idea of the kind of car he wanted to produce and call the Jordan Playboy.

The Playboy, like other cars in the Jordan line, was basically an "assembled" automobile. Most of its parts, including its 8-cylinder Continental engine, were made by outside manufacturers and then assembled in the Jordan plant. It was an excellent car, beautiful to look at, and very fast for its time.

But Ned Jordan is remembered not so much for his car as for the fresh, breezy advertisements he wrote about it. At a time when all other companies were advertising their cars with what he called "mechanical chatter," Ned Jordan never so much as mentioned a bolt, nut, or cotter pin. Instead, he appealed to the reader's emotions and the human love for adventure—an entirely new note in automobile advertising.

His famous ad, "Somewhere West of Laramie," didn't even show what the car looked like. It was illustrated by a rough sketch of a cowboy galloping beside a black object that only vaguely resembled a roadster with a windblown girl at the wheel. But the words Ned put in the ad tugged at the heartstrings and made the reader want to own a Playboy even if he had to mortgage his home to buy it.

"Somewhere west of Laramie there's a bronco-busting, steer-roping girl who knows what I'm talking about," he wrote. *"A lass whose face is brown with the sun . . . who loves the cross of the wild and the tame."* As for the car itself, he felt it was enough to say that it had *"a savor of laughter and lilt and light . . . a hint of old loves."* It was *"a brawny thing—yet a graceful thing for the sweep o' the Avenue."* He ended the ad by saying, *"Step into the Playboy—then start for the land of real living with the spirit of the lass who rides, lean and rangy, into the red horizon of a Wyoming twilight."*

These soaring poetic thoughts may sound corny to us today, but they sold a goodly number of Jordan Playboys. By 1931, however, when the lushest cars in the Jordan line carried $5,550 price tags, not even flowery phrases were able to persuade depression-pinched buyers to part with their money. The Jordan Motor Car Company went out of business.

1926/ *Pontiac*

Indian Chief Pontiac, head of the Ottawa tribe, never knew that someday there would be an American city—and an automobile, too—named after him. The colorful old chief went to his reward in the Happy Hunting Grounds more than 150 years before the brave Pontiac Chief of Sixes, with its chrome Indian-chief ornament on the radiator cap, made its bow at the New York Automobile Show in January, 1926.

The story of the Pontiac actually goes back to the Gay Nineties and the days of buggies and whip sockets. It was in 1893 that an enterprising young man by the name of Edward M. Murphy set himself up in the town of Pontiac, Michigan, as a builder of fine buggies and carriages.

In the early 1900s, he began to take an interest in the sputtering horseless carriages that occasionally appeared on the streets. Most people thought they were just a passing fad, but Murphy didn't. He bought the rights to a little 2-cylinder engine that ran backwards, equipped a section of his plant for building gas buggies, and hung up a sign announcing the birth of the Oakland Motor Car Company.

His 2-cylinder Oaklands didn't sell very well. People didn't like the idea of cranking the engine in the wrong direction.

In 1908 he started building 4-cylinder cars. They became widely acclaimed as good hill-climbers at a time when most cars had to be coaxed uphill in lowest gear. He built 278 Oaklands that year, and 1,035 the next. Then he sold his company, at a good profit, and Oakland became a part of the newly formed General Motors Corporation.

It was always known as a good car. In 1920, General Motors brought it out as a Six. It was the first light car to have an enclosed body, and by 1925 it had become one of the most popular cars built.

Just about then, the industry began to buzz with rumors that GM was planning to bring out a "companion" car to the Oakland, a car that would be "new from the blueprints up." The rumors were true. The car was the Pontiac.

The public was enthusiastic about the new Chief of Sixes. By the end of 1926, GM had built and sold 76,783 of them, setting an all-time first-year record. From then on, there was no stopping the Pontiac. Today, more than forty years later, it still ranks among the top best-sellers.

What about the Oakland, the spunky little car that started it all? In 1929, after twenty-two years of production, the millionth Oakland rolled off the line. But during the next few years, the car became so overshadowed by its brilliant running-mate that the end was in sight. It came, in 1932.

While the Oakland was never a "dog," the Pontiac was the tail that wagged it right out of existence —one of the few successful "companion" cars in history.

1927 / *La Salle*

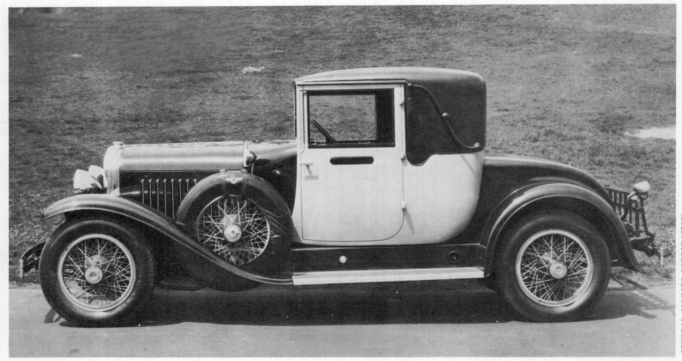

This is the story of how the La Salle became the first production car in automobile history to be completely designed from bumper to bumper by a professional stylist.

In the mid-1920s, one of the top executives of General Motors made a curious discovery while on a business trip to the West Coast. He was puzzled because so many of the Cadillacs on the streets of Los Angeles appeared to have "gone Hollywood." Instead of the drab colors and rather stodgy lines that were typical of the Cadillacs then being produced in Detroit, some of the cars he saw had the exciting flair of Isotta-Fraschinis, Hispano-Suizas, and other luxurious European cars.

It didn't take him long to get to the bottom of the mystery. He learned that more and more of the new Cadillacs shipped to the West Coast were being stripped down and fitted with custom-built bodies ordered by customers who wanted to drive a car that was distinctively "different." Most of the bodies were the creation of a young custom-coachwork designer named Harley J. Earl.

When Mr. Earl was approached, he finally agreed to come to Detroit as a styling consultant to Cadillac. His first task was to create a series of bodies for a new car that was to become an elegant young sister for the Cadillac line. It was to be called the La Salle.

Engineering design for the car had been under way since 1923. Basically, the La Salle was to be a slightly smaller version of the Cadillac itself. Its 75-hp V-8 engine was almost identical to the Cadillac's, except for smaller-bore cylinders.

While Harley Earl worked up sketches for La Salle bodies, the engineers continued their around-the-clock testing program on the new car. A stripped-down roadster was put through its paces on the proving-ground track. On a 10-hour run it turned in a blistering average speed of 95.2mph, which was pretty close to the record those days in the Indianapolis 500.

Everyone was delighted with the car's performance, and when the Earl-designed body styles became sheet-metal realities, GM knew it had succeeded in creating a motorcar worthy of being introduced as a companion car to the stately Cadillac.

The first sports cabriolet is an excellent example of how Harley Earl adapted his knowledge of custom coachwork to a mass-produced automobile. The close-coupled passenger compartment, the fender-mounted wire wheels, and the graceful proportions of the car's lines all combined to convince the industry that the stylists day had finally dawned.

The head of General Motors was so pleased with the appearance of the car that he asked Mr. Earl to form a new department for styling all GM cars.

In 1940—the year in which Harley Earl became the first stylist to be appointed a vice-president of an automobile corporation—the La Salle's honorable career as a runner-up to Cadillac came to an end. In the fourteen years of its production, 207,-764 of the cars were built.

75

1928/ Model A Ford

Early in 1927, word leaked out that the Ford Motor Company was going to make a lady out of Lizzie. The rumor was true. In May of that year the company announced that it was ending production of the popular Model T.

Many loyal Ford owners hated to see their beloved car disappear. Some of them wrote to Dearborn, "Say it isn't so!" A Boston businessman hurried to his local dealer and bought half a dozen of the last Model T's, so he would be sure of always having one as long as he lived.

In January, 1928, after months of secrecy, the handsome Model A, successor to the Tin Lizzie, was introduced with great fanfare in New York's old Madison Square Garden. Full-page advertisements in the newspapers heralded the long-awaited event. On the day of the showing, the police were called out to hold back the mobs clamoring for a look at the new Ford. Fifty thousand people eagerly placed orders and paid cash deposits on the new car. Elsewhere, in cities all across the country, the Model A was greeted with the same enthusiasm.

The wonder of it is that the company had waited so long to replace the out-of-date Model T. Henry Ford still felt it was the finest car being built, and until the bitter end kept insisting, "You can have any color you want, as long as it's black." But most of the Ford executives, including his son Edsel, knew it was high time for a change. Chevrolet and other auto manufacturers had been challenging Ford's leadership for a number of years with smarter-looking, more modern cars. Public favor was clearly swinging toward automobiles that offered comfort, beauty, and new engineering features, as well as utility.

In the new Model A, people found what they had been waiting for—a low-priced, good-looking car with modern features. Gone was the old-fashioned planetary transmission and its 3 pedals. The new car had a standard 3-speed transmission with a gearshift lever. Instead of a hand throttle mounted on the steering column, there was an accelerator on the floor. The gas tank, while still using gravity flow, was no longer under the driver's seat but inside the hood cowling. A new 40hp engine, with almost twice the power of the Model T's, gave the car a top speed of 65mph.

Best of all, it was a well-styled automobile. A number of body models were available and—surprise, surprise!—a wide choice of attractive colors.

The company had spent millions of dollars in retooling the factory to produce the Model A. But the venture paid off handsomely. Nearly 5 million Model A's were built and sold during the car's four-year life-span. Many of them still exist today, in good running order. And collectors lucky enough to own one of these great little cars seem to have the same affection for it as those who drove the Model A when it first came out, more than forty years ago.

1929 / *Plymouth*

In the summer of 1928, if you had been reading a certain Detroit newspaper carefully, you might have come across an inside-page rumor that an auto maker, who was not named, was planning to bring out a new low-priced car.

This was at a time when Henry Ford had completed his switchover from the Tin Lizzie to the spanking-new, fast-selling Model A. Anyone in his right mind must have known that Ford and Chevy had the market for low-priced cars pretty much to themselves. Who in the world, you might have wondered, could be so foolhardy as to buck these two automotive giants by offering the public still a third low-priced car!

Who indeed, it turned out, but Walter P. Chrysler—the up-and-coming auto wizard whose classy Chrysler Six had gotten off to a whirlwind start only four years before.

It was a month later, however, before the cat was out of the bag and the rumor became a reality. The name of the new car was Plymouth. People thronged to New York's Madison Square Garden and to the Chicago Coliseum to get a glimpse of it.

What they saw was a smart-looking car with a price tag of only $670 (for the coupé) and $690 for the 2-door sedan. But the Plymouth had a lot of things going for it besides price. Its name, for example, which had been chosen to suggest the honest, rugged qualities of the Pilgrims who had landed at Plymouth Rock. If Pilgrims were good, the Plymouth had to be good, too.

The car was powered by a high-compression 4-cylinder Silver Dome engine that delivered 45hp on regular gas and a top speed of 60mph. It had other features, too, that no one had ever seen before on a low-priced automobile, such as 4-wheel hydraulic brakes, balloon tires, a rubber engine mount, and a mysterious-sounding "body impulse neutralizer system" that was supposed to absorb road vibrations.

There was no doubt about it—the new Plymouth had the makings of a winner. The story goes that Chrysler himself wheeled one of the first Plymouths off the assembly line and drove it triumphantly over to show Henry Ford. The stern sage of Dearborn peered at it for a moment and said, "It looks like a good car, Walter, but you'll go broke trying to get into the low-price market. Chevrolet and ourselves have it sewed up."

But Ford was mistaken. In the months following its introduction, Chrysler sold 58,031 Plymouths. In 1929, the first full year of production, sales jumped to 93,613. A few years later, the Plymouth factory rolled its millionth automobile off the line —the first of well over 15 million Plymouths it was to produce over the next four decades. Walter P. Chrysler's David-and-Goliath gamble paid off handsomely, as he believed it would.

1930 / *Cadillac V-16*

In the company's early years, when other pioneer auto builders were debating whether to increase the number of their engine cylinders to 2 or even 4, Cadillac steadfastly stuck to its original idea: 1 cylinder. So, in 1930, it could be said of Cadillac, as in the cigarette TV commercial of more recent times, "You've come a long way, baby." For in January of that year, Cadillac made news by introducing America's first 16-cylinder production automobile.

The V-16 was the last word in luxury, comfort, and power. And it *should* have been, for it cost from $5,350 to $15,000, depending on which of its fifty custom-built Fleetwood body styles you wanted. The big, powerful car had a wheelbase of more than 12 feet—8 inches longer than the standard Cadillac V-8. Most of the models weighed better than 6,000 pounds—3 tons of handcrafted steel beauty on wheels.

The V-16 was a classic mechanical marvel. Its engine, built to Cadillac's exacting precision tolerances, consisted of 2 straight-8 cylinder blocks set at a 45° angle, both sharing the same crankcase. Even by standards of today's engines, it was a tremendous power package. With its 430-cubic-inch displacement, its power output was 185hp.

Cadillac proudly boasted of the V-16's "whispered hush" of smooth power and its instant response, which their engineers attributed to the simple principle of "multiplying total power and subdividing by 16." The engine's tiny 3-inch pistons had an amazingly short stroke. Each of the 16 pistons, as it fired, traveled a distance of only 4 inches to deliver its full power impulse. Another thing about the engine: if it needed tuning up, each bank of cylinders could be made to run independently, without the other. This enabled a mechanic to tune one bank while the other just pumped air.

Public enthusiasm for this most luxurious of custom-built motor cars was almost phenomenal when you consider that it was introduced just when the Great Depression was beginning to make itself felt.

Even so, by April, 1930, the first 1,000 V-16's had all been sold, and 1,887 more of them were produced by the end of the year. But in 1932, when all manufacturers of "prestige" automobiles were feeling the brunt of continuing hard times, Cadillac's production of the elegant V-16 dropped to 300, and by 1936 orders had hit an all-time low of only 50 units.

Nothing daunted, the company brought out an entirely new version of the V-16 in 1938. But even though a limited number of the cars were built up until 1940, it had then become clear that the multiple-cylinder, expensive masterpiece had had its day of glory. There just weren't enough millionaires around any more. The magnificent big car with the distinctive chrome V-16 monogram mounted between its massive 13-inch headlamps had reached the end of the road.

1931 / *Marmon 16*

WILLIAM R. GIBSON

The Marmon company was never a me-too, follow-the-leader builder of automobiles. It just happened that it was the second, and only company except Cadillac, to bring out a 16-cylinder automobile.

The history of this fine old Indianapolis company goes back to the year 1876, when it was known as a producer of milling machinery. Not until after the turn of the century, when the grandson of the founder became head of the company, did it begin to dabble seriously in machinery-on-wheels. In 1902, young Howard Marmon, wanting a better automobile than any he could find, decided to build his own. It had an air-cooled V-2 engine and was a good little car.

Convinced that the multiple-cylinder engine was the coming thing, Marmon designed a V-4 for the gas buggy he built the following year. Six friends wanted duplicates of the car. Encouraged by his success, he set aside a portion of his factory, in 1905, for building automobiles on a production basis.

Early Marmons were advanced cars for their day. One of them won a perfect score in the 1906 Glidden Tour. Other Marmons won many racing awards. Entered in the first Indy 500, one turned in a then-incredible 74.61mph average speed for the grueling distance.

Of the many magnificent cars built in the company's later years, one of the finest and least-known of great American automobiles was the Marmon 16, which was introduced in January, 1931. Its tremendous 491.8-cubic-inch engine had the greatest displacement of any motor then being built. With an output of 200hp at 3,400rpm, the awesome V-16 was the crowning glory of Howard Marmon's career. Its turbinelike smoothness became almost a legend among those who loved cars capable of spectacular performance. Each car was sold with a certificate stating that, ready for delivery, with full equipment, it had been tested out at over 100mph for at least 5 miles on the nearby Indianapolis Speedway.

The beauty of the car was as impressive as its performance. Priced at $5,000 and up, it came in 8 elegant body styles, most of which were created by Walter Dorwin Teague, the foremost industrial designer of the day. Its lines were clean and pleasing to the eye, uncluttered by gadgets and trim. The limited-edition Marmon 16 was truly a classic car.

Only about 500 of them were ever produced. A handful still exist, mostly in the hands of collectors. One, even now in almost daily use, has close to 200,000 miles on its odometer and is still going strong. Several others have clocked well over 100,000 miles.

The fact that the Marmon factory folded soon after it built the last of the great 16's is no reflection on this superb motorcar. The company failed simply because it made the mistake of trying to stay in a luxury market that was fading fast.

1932 / Duesenberg SJ

If any American motorcar ever deserved to be called great, it was the Big D. Because of its name, some people mistakenly thought of it as a German car. But Fred and Augie Duesenberg, although born in Germany, actually grew up in Iowa. It was in Indianapolis, starting in the 1920s, that the brothers achieved fame as builders of racing cars and the fabulous automobiles that bore their name.

The Duesenberg company did not build its own bodies, only the chassis. The bodies were designed and built to each customer's order. So it is not surprising that a Duesenberg usually cost from $14,000 to $25,000. It was a car only the very rich could afford. And what a car it was!

The most famous of all Duesenbergs—and one highly prized by classic-car collectors—was the Model SJ (S for "supercharged"), which was introduced in 1932. This "blown" version of the well-known Model J had a wheelbase of 142½ inches and weighed 2½ tons. Yet its huge supercharged straight-8 engine, with an incredible output of 320-hp, enabled the massive car to accelerate from a standstill to 100mph in 17 seconds. It had a top speed of 130mph and could clock over 100mph in *second* gear. Obviously, this beautiful beast of a car was not meant for the timid driver. It was a spectacular motorcar for spectacular people—wealthy sportsmen, royalty, and Hollywood celebrities.

For sheer luxury, as well as horsepower, the elegant "Duzy" was unsurpassed. From its pre-cisely-machined aluminum pistons and connecting rods to the soft imported leathers and fine broadcloth upholstery of its superb custom-built bodies, everything about the car was just about as perfect as human skill and craftsmanship could make it.

No detail was too small to be overlooked. Its dashboard was a wonder to behold, with almost as many dials and signal lights as the flight deck of a Boeing 727. In addition to all the standard instruments you'd expect to find, there was a tachometer, an altimeter-barometer, a split-second stopwatch chronometer, and a brake-pressure gauge. Its cluster of computerlike warning lights included one that flashed red every 750 miles (a reminder to change the oil), another that glowed once every 1,500 miles (time to check the water level in the battery), and still another that indicated whether the proper amount of lubricating oil was getting to all vital points in the chassis.

The last Duesenbergs were built in the late 1930s, when fewer and fewer people could afford to pay a king's ransom for a motorcar. There are still several hundred of them around. Most of them are maintained in mint condition by their proud owners and run as sweetly today as when they were brand-new, almost forty years ago. To find one in even less than perfect condition—perhaps tucked away in some old barn and forgotten—would be like discovering the Kohinoor diamond.

1933 / *Silver Arrow*

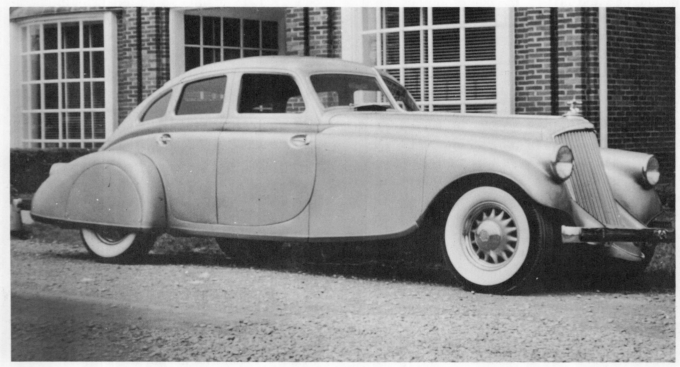

Duesenberg was not the only maker of luxury cars to find the going tough in the lean depression years of the early thirties. Packard and Cadillac were beginning to feel the pinch, too.

And the Pierce-Arrow company, with its long and glorious reputation, was in deep trouble in spite of having recently merged with Studebaker, the venerable manufacturer of medium-priced automobiles in South Bend, Indiana. Studebaker, as the parent company in the merger, was eager to round out its line of cars with a high-priced marque such as the Pierce-Arrow.

The two companies decided to take one last desperate gamble by bringing out a very special limited-edition car: a Pierce-Arrow V-12 chassis with an ultra-modern streamlined body. The price tag of the new Silver Arrow was to be $10,000. The target date for delivery was New Year's Day, 1933, in time for its introduction at the New York Automobile Show.

One night in October, 1932, five V-12 chassis were covered with tarpaulins and secretly shipped from Buffalo to Studebaker's experimental engineering shops. Here the new bodies were to be painstakingly built by hand, according to sketches already agreed upon. But with only three months to go, meeting the deadline seemed an impossibility.

Everything else was sidetracked in order to accomplish the task. A group of about thirty skilled craftsmen—wood workers, metal finishers, painters, and trimmers—pitched in and worked almost around the clock, as if their lives were at stake. All of the car's metal panels, including the roof, had to be hammered out by hand over carved wooden forms. What a job it was! The fact that the first Silver Arrow *was* completed and shipped to New York on schedule was a tribute to one of the most amazing feats of teamwork imaginable.

Except for its traditional fender-mounted headlamps, the beautiful tan-and-brown Silver Arrow bore little resemblance to any Pierce-Arrow ever made. The streamlined fender line flowed in bold relief past the doors, sweeping downward to merge with the car's teardrop rear end. The massive doors of its double-shelled body were almost 12 inches thick, with concealed hinges. The spare wheels were tucked out of sight in lockers inside the front fenders. The car had no running boards. Its rich interior was finished in hand-rubbed curly maple, with leather-trimmed broadcloth. A final touch, for the benefit of back-seat passengers, was a miniature instrument panel in the rear compartment, complete with an electric clock and speedometer.

The 175hp Silver Arrow, with a top speed of 115-mph, was quite a car, but it came too late, and at the wrong time, to cure the lingering illness of the two companies that teamed up to produce it.

1934 / *Chrysler Airflow*

Airflow CHRYSLER
AMERICA'S NEW CHAMPION
CLOSED STOCK CAR
From
1 MILE to
2000 MILES
CONTEST BOARD
AAA
SANCTION No 3022
Official
1 MILE
95.7 M.P.H.
HOLDER OF
72 OFFICIAL RECORDS

CHRYSLER CORPORATION.

At the end of a summer day in 1927, as the chief engineer at Chrysler was driving home, he saw a formation of military planes approaching from over the horizon, coming in for a letdown at nearby Selfridge Field.

As he pondered their smooth, effortless flight, he asked himself, "Why hasn't anyone ever thought of designing a car that could take advantage of air currents and wind forces, instead of using so much of its power to push its boxlike shape through a solid wall of resisting air? That's why airplanes are streamlined. Why not automobiles?"

Eager to find out if this idea made any sense, he constructed a simple, rectangular wind tunnel and began experimenting with miniature scale models of automobiles. Using linseed oil and lampblack to trace a visual record of the way the air flowed around the models, he and his engineers made a startling discovery: a conventional automobile running backward encountered less air resistance than it did when running forward!

Convinced that automobiles were all running in the wrong direction, aerodynamically, they got busy designing models in which everything was reversed —not only the shape of the car but its weight distribution as well.

One day, just for fun, they took an ordinary Chrysler sedan and switched the steering and drive mechanism from front to rear. When they drove it through the streets of Detroit, traffic cops rubbed their eyes and reached for their whistles. "The car that ran backwards" didn't prove anything, of course. It was simply a publicity stunt to let people know that something big was cooking at Chrysler.

The throngs who attended the 1934 Automobile Show finally got a glimpse of what had been cooking. After years of experimentation, Chrysler was now introducing its new Airflow car. It was the talk of the show.

Most people thought the car was rather funny-looking. They hesitated about buying a car that looked so different from conventional automobiles, even though they had to admit that its design probably made sense.

The Chrysler Airflow had a snubby "waterfall" hood and grille, from which the fenders seemed to curve out gracefully instead of being tacked on. The rear end of the car tapered to a teardrop shape and the rear wheel openings were skirted to reduce air drag.

Because of its unique design and several important engineering firsts, the car had terrific performance. In trial runs on the Great Salt Desert in Utah, it copped 72 new stock car records, including a mile at 95.7mph and an average speed of 90.04mph over a 500-mile course.

Although the car made headlines, it was not a success. The public wasn't ready for a car that looked like that. So, at the end of its 1937 model year, after only 29,918 of them had been built and sold, the Chrysler Airflow quietly backed out of the picture, running forward.

1935/ Auburn 851

Most classic-car buffs agree that this sleek 2-seater was the finest car ever built in the thirty-six-year history of the Auburn company. One thing is certain: it was a far cry from the first chain-driven gas buggy built in 1900 by the two Eckhart brothers in their Indiana carriage works—or anything they were able to produce later on.

In 1924, after almost a quarter of a century of building Auburn automobiles, the Eckhart brothers found themselves in desperate straits. Their factory was then producing only 6 cars a day, and even those were not selling. The company finally failed, and a group of Chicago bankers took over. The first thing they did was to hire a new general manager—a dynamic young man by the name of E. L Cord. Things started to hum. Within two years, the company was showing a million-dollar profit, and Cord—by then known as the wonder boy—became its president, at the age of thirty-two.

Cord added several of the country's top stylists to his staff, as well as the famed speed king, Ab Jenkins. Over the next ten years, the company turned out a number of spectacular cars. The supercharged 851 Speedster was one of them—probably the greatest.

With a long low hood, small cockpit, teardrop fenders, rakish boatlike tail, and chrome exhaust stacks protruding from the side of its engine compartment, the car's styling gave it a racy, powerful look. And it lived up to its appearance.

The 851's power plant was a straight-8 by Lycoming, the well-known builders of aircraft engines. Equipped with supercharger, this muscled-up job turned out 150hp at 2,900rpm. And the car could really move! On the dash of each 851 Speedster there was a plaque, signed either by Ab Jenkins or his teammate Wade Morton, certifying that the car had been tested out, before delivery, at over 100-mph. Ab Jenkins himself, driving a stock 851, had previously set a record at Bonneville salt flats by clocking an average speed of 103mph *for 500 miles.*

The car had a 3-speed transmission, but by turning a little knob-lever on the steering column, the driver had at his command a selective 6-speed gearshift, which was activated simply by depressing the clutch pedal.

Each Auburn 851 was virtually built by hand, but it was priced well below what people would have been willing to pay for a custom-built automobile. It is said that the company lost several hundred dollars on every one it sold, which is not the way an auto manufacturer can afford to operate for very long. Only about 500 of the elegant speedsters were ever produced.

By the end of 1936, with its back to the wall because of dwindling sales on its other automobiles as well, the Auburn company went out of business, and the 851 Speedster, a truly sensational motorcar, breathed its last.

1936/ *Lincoln Zephyr*

A wise man, and a prudent company, can often learn a lot by observing the mistakes of others. In this case, Chrysler was the guinea pig. If its 1934 Airflow had been a howling success, perhaps Ford would have gone ahead with the experimental streamlined car it exhibited at the Chicago World's Fair in 1933. But public lack of enthusiasm for the Airflow made it clear that people were not ready for a car that was too far-out and radical in its styling.

So a special group of designers in Ford's Lincoln division was asked to go back to the drawing board and create a streamlined medium-priced car that would be new and exciting, yet have un-Airflow styling. The result was the 1936 Lincoln Zephyr, with its tapered-V radiator grille, flat hood, fender-mounted headlights, and teardrop rear end. It was a striking, good-looking car. So good that New York's Museum of Modern Art later called it "the first successfully streamlined car in America."

The Lincoln Zephyr was the first car costing under $3,000 to have a V-12 engine. Designed by Lincoln engineers and precision-built in the Lincoln plant, the engine had a small bore and stroke—only $2\frac{3}{4} \times 3\frac{3}{4}$ inches—and delivered 110hp. It was a lot of engine for a car of that size. The high ratio of engine power to car weight soon gained the Zephyr a reputation for having just about the fastest rate of acceleration of any production car then being made.

Aside from its magnificent engine and advanced styling, the car also made news because it was the first to use the "unitized" principle of construction. The body and frame were one—a rugged *unit* of light steel girders, like the trusses in a bridge. The steel panels of the body—top, sides, and bottom—were welded directly to these steel girders, instead of being just assembled separately to form a shell that could be dropped onto a chassis.

The Lincoln Zephyr's aerodynamic styling met with a happier fate than that of the ill-starred Chrysler Airflow. People liked the car. It sold well as long as it was kept in production.

Perhaps its greatest, and least-known, claim to fame is the story of how it suddenly became the Cinderella of motorcars and the direct ancestor of America's most famous classic car.

When Edsel Ford, the president of the company, asked his stylists to build him a "personal" car with a "continental" flair, they chose a 1939 Lincoln Zephyr chassis as their takeoff point. They lowered the height of the body, lengthened its hood, threw away its running boards, tacked a spare tire on back—and *presto!*—the first Lincoln Continental was born.

You will find the story told in more detail when you come to the year 1940.

1937/ *Cord 812*

The Auburn automobile may have reached the end of the road in 1936, but the fabulous E. L. (Erret Lobban) Cord had not. His distinctive "coffin-nosed" Cord 812 was one of the most glamorous automobiles to appear on the American scene in the late 1930s.

In many ways, the Cord was years ahead of its time. Its styling, the creation of designer Gordon Buehrig, was terrific. Low and clean-lined, with a smartly canted windshield, it was a pleasing combination of curves and angles. Since it was a front-wheel-drive car, the stepdown floor of its 2-passenger cockpit was completely flat, lacking the usual humped-up drive-shaft tunnel. Nor were there any running boards. The massive rounded front fenders extended well beyond the recessed nose of the car, giving it the eager look of a 100mph speedster (which it was) even when standing still.

Another styling first—not to be seen again until it appeared on certain cars in the late 1960s—was its fully retractable headlamps, which could be made to emerge from the fenders by turning 2 small cranks on the instrument panel. The car had 4 gleaming outside exhaust stacks, and its convertible top could be stowed out of sight, adding to the keen, racy appearance of its overall design.

Although beautifully styled, the early 812's were not the mechanical marvels they should have been. They tended to overheat at cruising speed, and the transmission had an annoying habit of popping out of gear every now and then. These faults were corrected in later models of the series.

Powered by a supercharged Lycoming V-8, the "blown" Cord developed 170hp. Its official speed record of 107.6mph was to remain unbroken by any other production car for the next fifteen years.

Priced at almost $4,000, in those lean years when you could buy a big Buick for less than $900, the lovely Cord enjoyed a short but glorious lifetime. It was awarded a Gold Medal in Paris for the beauty of its design, and New York's Museum of Modern Art selected it as one of the ten outstanding cars of all time, more than a decade after it first appeared.

But in spite of medals and awards, the Cord was not rewarded by the general public acceptance it deserved. Only about 3,000 of them were built. But its fame endures. It is one of the most prized of all classic cars.

A Cord 812 in good condition is usually worth considerably more today than its original cost. Members of the select Auburn-Cord-Duesenberg Club meet once a year in Indiana, where they proudly display and compare their treasured cars. They say, and others agree, that the Cord never really died and never will.

1938 / *Mercury*

On November 4, 1938, Henry Ford and his son Edsel announced the birth of a new automobile—the Mercury Eight. Following industry custom, they jumped the gun by a couple of months and designated the newcomer as a 1939 model.

The car excited great public interest, especially among loyal Ford owners who wanted a car larger than the regular Ford V-8, but less expensive than the somewhat fancier Lincoln Zephyr. Priced from $894 to $994, depending on the model, the new Mercury filled the gap perfectly.

It was the first car in Ford history to be designed completely by "inside" company stylists, from original drawings to clay model to finished product. Its smart V-shaped grille and teardrop streamlining showed that the designers had been strongly influenced by the basic styling of the handsome Zephyr. The resemblance was intentional.

There was no question about it: the new Mercury was a lot of car for the money. It was powered by a larger, beefed-up version of the popular Ford V-8 engine, with a displacement of 239 cubic inches and an output of 95hp at 3,600rpm. Proving-ground tests showed it could accelerate from a standing stop to 60mph in 13.3 seconds, with a top speed of 90mph. All good numbers in 1938.

The car had a wheelbase of 116 inches and an overall length of 196 inches. Because of its double drop-frame construction, the sedan was one of the roomiest cars on the market. Its wide seats, front and rear, provided ample hip room for 6 passengers, instead of 5.

The Mercury was marked for success from the very start. In the two months following its introduction, 10,366 were sold. During its first full model year, 73,013 more rolled off the line.

Even by today's standards, the early Mercurys were fine automobiles. By 1938 standards, they were terrific. An interesting publicity photo, taken at the time of the car's introduction, shows a Mercury squatting on an airport runway under the nose of what was then the hottest plane in the American Airlines fleet—the flagship Mercury. The photo caption reminds us of the airline's boast that its twin-engined Douglas DC-3 could zoom from "coast-to-coast with only four stops." Obviously, airliners and Mercurys too have come a long way since those days.

In more recent years, ever since the Ford company resumed its interest in stock-car racing, the Mercury has been a consistent winner. With driver Parnelli Jones at the wheel, a Mercury broke the all-time record in the 41st Pikes Peak Hill Climb, and followed that with winning ways at various tracks around the country, including Riverside's rugged Golden Gate 400 grind.

People who have owned and driven one Mercury after another, over the past thirty years, say they have never known a really bad Mercury model. That's high praise for any marque, including the Big M.

1939 / *Packard 120*

This beautiful convertible made its appearance on the Packard company's fortieth anniversary. It was called the 120 because the brake horsepower rating of its Packard-built straight engine was 120hp.

A brilliant motorcar, both in styling and performance, it was priced at only $1,390 "f.o.b. Detroit." A lot of Packard admirers who formerly had been content merely to "Ask the Man Who Owns One" now found that they could afford to "*be* the man who owns one." In fact, 17,647 people became proud Packard 120 owners during the 1939 model year.

Probably its low price, and the fact that so many of them were built, are two reasons why some present-day Packard fans don't become terribly excited about the car as a collector's item. In their opinion, it lacks the appeal of the more expensive, more exclusive, classic Packards. But fortunately, the public felt otherwise in 1939. The 120 was a successful car, and continued to be for the next two years.

The Packard company was also building big luxury cars in 1939, although that was to be the last year in which cars like the fabulous Packard Twelve were produced.

The Twelve was a long, luxurious car that weighed over 2½ tons. Yet the seemingly ponderous vehicle could accelerate from a crawl to 30mph *in high gear* in 8.5 seconds. The secret of its lively performance was its superb precision-built V-12 Packard engine, which was a direct descendent of Jesse Vincent's earlier Twin Six.

No owner of a Packard Twelve ever had to "break in" his new car, as had to be done with most automobiles then. Packard engineers themselves saw to the breaking in of each car, before delivery. Following assembly of the engine, there were countless factory inspections. Then each Packard Twelve was put through a 250-mile series of test runs on the Packard proving grounds, including a workout on the 2½-mile oval speedway and periodic tune-up stops at the adjacent engineering laboratory. At the end of its break-in trials, each mighty Twelve was as finely honed as a 17-jewel Swiss watch.

Naturally, it was an expensive car. You paid up to $6,880 for one, depending on the model. Only 446 of these limited-edition Packards were produced in 1939, before the line was discontinued.

One of them was a special-order Twelve built as a parade car for Franklin D. Roosevelt. The huge, 7-passenger custom body by Dietrich had bulletproof windshield and windows that could withstand a direct hit from a 50-caliber machine gun. This historic car now reposes in the Antique Auto Museum at Larz Anderson Park, in Brookline, Massachusetts. It is not for sale.

But if you should happen to find one of the great 1939 Packard 120's looking for a home, don't pass it up.

1940/ *Lincoln Continental*

When Henry Ford's only son, Edsel, was still in his teens, one of his most prized possessions was a scrapbook containing his collection of photographs and sketches of the automobiles he liked best. Many of his favorites were European cars.

The boy grew up. Eventually, he succeeded his father as president of the Ford Motor Company. When that happened, he was able to make good use of his keen interest in the styling of automobiles. Some of his happiest moments were those he spent with his friends in the company's styling department, discussing new ideas. About once a year, the designers would build a special prototype car for his personal use, based on sketches they developed together.

In September, 1938, upon his return from a trip to Europe, he showed his stylists some rough sketches he had brought back with him and asked them if they would build him a special "strictly continental" convertible like the one shown in the sketches. The car was built and was promptly shipped to Florida for him to drive during his winter vacation.

The chassis of the beautiful prototype was that of a standard Lincoln Zephyr, with certain modifications. The result was a custom-built convertible unlike any ever seen before. The car, powered by a jewelled V-12 engine, had an impressive overall length of 210 inches and a height of only 62 inches.

Not only was it longer and lower than any car on the road, but it had no chrome strips or decorative devices to detract from the pleasing simplicity of its design. With its extra-long hood, short rear deck, and gracefully curving fenders, the car was a delight to the eye. The final touch was its "continental" wheel-mount at the rear, a European styling feature from which it derived its name, the Lincoln Continental.

The car created a sensation wherever it was seen in the Palm Beach area near Edsel Ford's winter home. More than two hundred people admired it so much, the story goes, that they insisted on giving its owner a blank-check order for a car just like it.

One day Mr. Ford called his Dearborn office, requesting that a second prototype be built—one that would be suitable for production in limited numbers. The engineers and stylists got busy. The first Lincoln Continentals to be made available to the public were formally introduced during the New York and Los Angeles auto shows the following October, for the 1940 model year.

Every Continental produced during the following few years was virtually custom-built, each hand-crafted with loving care. It was truly a limited-edition automobile. An average of less than 1,000 were built each year. The last of the original Lincoln Continentals was produced in 1948.

1941 / *Packard Clipper*

This was the year that marked the last chapter in the story of the classic Packard motorcar. Only a few hundred of the big luxurious models were still being built. The famous broad-shouldered vertical radiator grille—a Packard trademark ever since the car emerged from its horseless-carriage days—was soon to disappear forever, except as a treasured relic of the glorious past.

The eagerly awaited "new look" by Packard turned out to be an entirely redesigned automobile. Called the Clipper 8, it was introduced in March, 1941. Priced at only $1,305, it could scarcely be considered a luxury motorcar. And, unlike the classic old Packards, it had a chassis unsuited to special-order coachwork that might have upgraded it into the category of its costly custom-built fore-runners.

The Clipper was well received by the public, but it was not destined to go down in history as one of the truly great Packards. There was a jinx on it. Even its name became an unexpected source of embarrassment to the Packard company. Pan-American World Airways, it seemed, had previously adopted the name Clipper for its globe-girdling airliners. They objected to the idea of a four-wheeled vehicle sharing the name, and threatened court action if it were not dropped. But eventually the matter was forgotten.

A much more serious threat to the new-born Packard Clipper was the fact that war clouds were beginning to darken the horizon. The government had already asked all auto makers to cut back on the use of steel by curtailing their car production schedules. Packard, of course, met this request. Then, in February, 1942, Washington really lowered the boom, decreeing that the production of civilian automobiles cease altogether. The Clipper assembly lines closed down, and its manufacturing dies were put in mothballs.

The Packard company, now fully committed to the war effort, swung into a crash production program on 12-cylinder Rolls-Royce aircraft engines and Packard 12-cylinder marine engines for navy PT boats.

During the Clipper's brief prewar lifetime, less than 50,000 of the cars were produced. One of the most memorable examples was a one-of-a-kind, hand-built experimental Clipper convertible that was never unveiled to the public. This stunning styling-studio creation, if it still existed today, would be worth its weight in gold to a collector of Packard cars. But when it became apparent that production facilities for the Clipper and all other automobiles were to be converted to the manufacture of war matériel, the Packard engineers sadly consigned the lone Clipper convertible to the proving grounds, where it was literally run to death.

1942 / Ford

The 1942 Ford sedan had the sad distinction of being the last civilian automobile built before World War II. Few cars ever started life so full of promise and met so swift a fate.

It was a rather handsome car, with clean styling, but it offered very little that was new in the way of engineering features. Time was growing too short for that. Nevertheless, Dearborn headquarters proudly heralded it as "the finest car ever built by the Ford Motor Company," and with more truth than anyone then realized, proclaimed that "there never was a better time to buy a Ford!"

The only hint of darker days to come was the company's explanation that "because of defense requirements, some new materials have replaced old ones in the car, but in every case, the new is equal to, or better than, the old." Which was another way of saying that tons of steel and other strategic metals that formerly went into automobiles were now going into tanks, army trucks, guns and ammunition, airplanes and aircraft engines, and all the other complex equipment that man in his infinite wisdom had devised for waging twentieth-century warfare.

On February 10, 1942, the Ford Motor Company and the rest of the auto industry shut down their assembly lines. From that date until the end of the war, no new civilian cars were built. Instead, from the Ford plants alone, came 656,400 huge B-24

Liberator bombers, 57,000 aircraft engines, and 278,000 wartime Jeeps.

It is hard to imagine, if you were not around during those bleak days, what it was like for "a nation on wheels" suddenly to discover it no longer had wheels, except secondhand ones, with no new wheels in sight. The price of used cars in good running condition went sky-high. Cars that were beginning to wheeze and break down were eagerly bought up by junk dealers as scrap metal for the yawning blast furnaces of a country now involved in total war.

Even if the old family crate was in pretty good shape mechanically, you couldn't buy tires for it unless you had a job that was "essential to the war effort." To conserve our dwindling supply of tread-worn tires still in use, the national speed limit was set at 40mph, then reduced to 35mph. Travel was restricted to a minimum, and to keep it that way, the government issued gasoline ration books. The basic allowance was two gallons of gasoline a week, except for certain types of "necessary" car use, in which cases a car owner could apply for extra ration stamps. Driving for pleasure was definitely out.

Unable to buy new automobiles, Americans got along as best they could with what they had, which often was nothing at all. During the war years, the humble little vehicle known as the Jeep had the whole automobile industry show to itself. **105**

1943–1946 / Jeep

FORD MOTOR COMPANY.

KAISER JEEP CORPORATION.

More than half a million of these short-coupled utility cars were built during the war. Known as the G-P vehicle—for "general purpose"—its initials inspired the nickname Jeep and the English language gained a new word.

A famous World War II cartoon by Bill Mauldin showed a grieving cavalry sergeant standing with his back to his Jeep, one hand over his eyes, the other pointing a .45 revolver at his beloved vehicle, which had suffered combat damage beyond repair. The sergeant was about to put it out of its "misery."

The cartoon had no caption. It needed none, for the artist's pen by itself had captured the feeling of affection countless thousands of GI's had for the rugged little 4-wheel-drive vehicle.

The powerful 4-cylinder car was originally intended as a replacement for the motorcycle-and-sidecar of the First World War. But its usefulness went far beyond relaying messages and running reconnaissance missions.

The Jeep carried men and supplies over the sands of Africa, through the mountains of Italy and the jungles of the South Pacific. In remote outposts, wherever U.S. servicemen and their allies were stationed, the Jeep was part of the action. It penetrated shell-torn terrain to rescue the wounded. Armed with recoilless rifles and machine guns, it served as a miniature tank. It was used as a command car by generals, it towed trailers, it parked fighter planes on the strip, and more than once, it served as a chaplain's crude altar in the field. Its record was a glorious one.

After the war, the Jeep discarded its drab olive paint and appeared in bright new colors as an all-purpose civilian vehicle. Mothers began to use Jeeps to go shopping and to lug the kids to school. Their husbands found them ideal workhorses for plowing snowdrifts, digging postholes, and for driving to inaccessible spots on hunting and fishing trips. If there was any job a car was not supposed to do, or any place it was not supposed to go, the Jeep did it.

By this time, the ever-popular G-P had become known officially as the Universal Jeep. It was just as tough as ever, even though it was sometimes painted baby blue, bright red, or a smart oyster white. But however gay it may have looked, under its thick steel skin it was still the beloved old G-P.

1947 / *Studebaker*

RAYMOND LOEWY.

This unusual automobile—the first "all new" car to be produced after the war—had a family tree whose roots went back more than a hundred years, to the 1852 blacksmith shop established by Clem and Henry Studebaker in South Bend, Indiana.

When not too busy shoeing horses, the Studebaker brothers found time to build a few wagons. The small two-man shop soon grew into a business employing two hundred skilled workmen. It wasn't long before sturdy Studebaker wagons and elegant Studebaker buggies and carriages became known across the land as the best that money could buy.

Seeing how things were booming, another brother, known as J.M., came into the firm to lend a hand; then along came brother Peter and brother Jacob. In 1869, rightly claiming to be "the world's largest manufacturer of highway vehicles," they formed the Studebaker Brothers Manufacturing Company.

Although the Brothers Five continued to build wagons and fashionable "surreys with fringe on top" for many years, they realized at the turn of the century that the newfangled horseless carriage might be the coming thing. In 1902, the company produced the first self-propelled Studebaker vehicle —a neat little electric runabout. This was followed by 2-cylinder gasoline-powered auto buggies, and then by 4-cylinder touring cars that cost $3,000 (plus another $150 for a collapsible top).

Now big and prosperous, the company was reorganized as the Studebaker Corporation of America. For the next half century it was a major independent automobile manufacturer and one of the industry's best-known companies. Over this period it turned out millions of fine cars.

Among its most-talked-about automobiles was the sleek car designed by the noted stylist Raymond Loewy, which made its appearance in 1947. Known as the 5-passenger Champion coupé, the car featured distinctive wrap-around rear windows. Its 2 wide, curved rear windows were flanked on either side by an extra "rear-quarter" window. Lacking conventional metal rear-quarter panels, the car had total 360° visibility.

Of course, folks were bound to make a few jokes about it. One wag said it reminded him of a "double-ended ferryboat." Other people, when they saw it, would ask, "Is it coming or going?" But almost everybody had to admit that its revolutionary wrap-around windows were a pretty wonderful idea.

The "coming-and-going" automobile proved to be a popular car and sold well. Since it was really new, rather than a prewar car with a face-lifting job, this Studebaker gave the company a good headstart before its chief competitors, the Big Three, got their postwar assembly lines rolling.

1948 / *Tucker*

AUTOMOTIVE HISTORY COLLECTION. DETROIT PUBLIC LIBRARY.

The engineers and designers who teamed up soon after World War II to create this extraordinary automobile used to refer to it affectionately, among themselves, as the Tin Goose. It was truly a revolutionary car, with styling and engineering features that were far ahead of their time.

It started out as a dream car conceived in the brilliant mind of a man named Preston Tucker. Many of the men who helped him make his dream a reality had formerly been aircraft engineers and designers. They knew he was deadly serious when he insisted that he wanted them to build "a completely new kind of car," designed with utter disregard for Detroit's traditional ideas of what an automobile should be like.

And that was exactly what the rear-engine Tucker turned out to be. No one had ever seen anything like it. Although its power plant was originally a Franklin air-cooled helicopter engine, this idea was discarded in favor of a flat 6-cylinder engine consisting of a double bank of 3 opposed cylinders. This light aluminum engine, with a displacement of 335 cubic inches, developed 150hp and gave the streamlined car a top speed of 120mph. The Tucker could move from zero to 100mph in only 33 seconds.

The test engineers, lacking a proving ground on which to put their torpedolike car through its paces, used to make their high-speed runs on the highway from Chicago to Kankakee—until state troopers, unable to catch up with the Tucker in their 105mph squad cars, filed a complaint. So the company rented the Indianapolis Speedway for its shakedown runs.

The Tucker, among other things, was the first real wide-track automobile. Instead of the customary 56-inch tread, it had a front-wheel spread of 63 inches, with 65 inches in the rear. Because of Preston Tucker's obsession with safety, the car had disc brakes, independent 4-wheel suspension, a windshield that "popped out" forward upon impact, and a fully padded dash and interior.

One of the most distinguishing things about the car, aside from its far-out aerodynamic styling, was the single "Cyclops" headlamp centered above the grille. This nose-mounted driving light had a fixed beam, while the 2 side headlamps were "steerable," beaming their lights in the direction in which the wheels were being turned.

Years were to pass before very many of the motoring safeguards engineered into the Tucker were to appear in other American production cars —and some of them haven't yet, in spite of their proven worth.

If an automobile ever deserved to be called "the car of the future," it was the fabulous Tucker. Now, sadly enough, it is remembered as "the car that might have been." Only 50 of them were ever built. Following a long and involved court battle over financial matters, the company folded at the end of its first year of production.

1949 / *Jeepster*

Just as they made a lady out of Lizzie with the Model A Ford, the tough little workaday Jeep got a slick beauty treatment, twenty years later, when the Willys company brought it out as a smart, sporty convertible called the Jeepster.

It was a handsome 4-passenger vehicle with horizontal chrome bars across its grille, hooded headlamps, and a slightly rakish windshield. Its beltline dipped gently from the base of the front pillar, with a "hop-up" profile starting at the rear passenger compartment. In spite of its squared-off fenders, which were in the Jeep styling tradition, the car had a saucy, clean-lined look.

Unlike its all-purpose cousin, the Jeepster was only a rear-wheel-drive automobile. It had no transfer gearbox that would enable its driver to link its drive shaft to the front axle for 4-wheel drive. With its short 104-inch wheelbase, it was a "cute" car, and nimble, too. It was powered by a 4-cylinder Willys engine that delivered 63hp at 4000rpm. Equipped with overdrive, which reduced engine revolutions by 30 percent, it was a miser on fuel.

The Jeepster was a popular automobile. Why it was taken out of production after three short years is something of a mystery. Perhaps it was because when people buy a Jeep-built vehicle, they want everything the name stands for, including 4-wheel drive.

In 1963, the original Willys company became the present-day Kaiser-Jeep Corporation. The first new car to come off the assembly lines was a big brother of the time-proven Jeep, called the Wagoneer. It was a family-size all-steel station wagon that combined style and comfort with the "go-anywhere" advantages of 4-wheel drive.

And then a car called the Jeepster appeared on the scene again. The lively newcomer bore a striking resemblance to its 1949 namesake, although its styling was somewhat more angular and it was shorter, by 3 inches. In the company's sales literature, the car was usually shown with the driver's big dog occupying the rear seat, which was a hint that it was now a 3-passenger car. The rear seat was not wide enough to accommodate 2 persons.

The new version of the Jeepster was a much more powerful car than the original one. It had an overhead-valve V-6 engine that delivered 160hp at 4200rpm. The staunch "do-anything" convertible caught the public's fancy from the start. It may have looked something like a dragster, but at heart it was still a Jeep. You could even hook a snowplow on front and install a stationary power takeoff unit on the rear end for doing chores.

As long as there are automobiles, there will probably always be a Jeep in some form or other, and as honest as they come. A lot of people hope so.

113

1950 / *Nash Rambler*

It's hard to tell just when the great American horsepower race really started. In a way, it was back in the early 1900s, when pioneer gas-buggy builders went from 1- to 2- to 4-cylinder engines.

Naturally, as bigger and more powerful engines were developed, cars themselves kept getting bigger and heavier. There finally came a time when you could buy a luxurious V-8 or V-16 sedan with an overall length of 20 feet. People who did sometimes had to build extensions on their garages to accommodate the behemoths. As cars grew bigger, they also became more expensive to buy and to operate. Yet, over the years, Detroit firmly believed this was the kind of automobile the motoring public wanted.

One auto company, in Kenosha, Wisconsin, wasn't quite so sure. Perhaps, reasoned Nash Motors, the big-car, big-horsepower race had gotten out of hand, and the time had come to "think small." It was a gamble, of course, but bringing out a good-looking small car might be the magic formula that would pep up dwindling Nash sales.

So in March, 1950, the company crossed its fingers for luck and dared to buck the big-car trend by introducing a handsome convertible on a short, 100-inch wheelbase. It was America's first compact car, and to get a name for it, the company reached back almost fifty years into its own history. . . .

It was in 1902 that a bicycle-maker named Thomas B. Jeffery built his first gasoline-powered buggy, in Kenosha. He called the little runabout the Rambler. For many years it was one of America's best-known automobiles. Then, in 1916, the Jeffery company changed hands. It was taken over by Charles W. Nash, a former farm boy who had risen to the presidency of General Motors and then resigned so that he could build a car under his own name. Thus, the 1950 Nash Rambler was a historic car on two counts: its ancestry and its small size.

It was a smartly styled small car. People also liked its low price and the money-saving economy of its peppy 6-cylinder engine. The car could be driven 25 to 30 miles on a gallon of gas.

By 1953, the company was turning out Nash Ramblers at the rate of 150,000 a year. But it had problems, and found itself going deeper and deeper into the red. In 1954, in order to survive, it merged with American Motors Corporation.

The compact was kept in production for another two years. Then, as the Volkswagen and other small foreign cars skyrocketed in popularity, it became clear that the public had fallen out of love with American compacts, at least for the time being.

So the name Nash was dropped and the car became simply the Rambler—a bigger, 120hp car on a longer, 108-inch wheelbase. But give the little Nash Rambler "A" for effort. It *almost* made it.

1951 / *Hudson Hornet*

Introduced by Hudson in 1951, the "fabulous Hornet" was probably the most newsworthy car the company had produced since the days of the famed Hudson Super Six.

Not because of its styling. It was an impressively low car, but much too tubby. Viewed head-on, the Hornet's massive grille, surmounted by twin headlight lenses, vaguely suggested a bug-eyed prehistoric monster advancing with gaping jaws. It is doubtful that it ever occurred to the Hudson stylists, when they designed the car, that anyone would conjure up such an image of their beloved creation. Actually, Packard and several other cars had almost identical front-end styling that year. It was what Detroit thought the public wanted.

The Hornet was destined to make news, not for its grace and questionable beauty, but for the lethal sting of its high-compression, 145hp, 6-cylinder engine. When the first production cars were put through test runs on the track, the results came through loud and clear. Hudson had a winner—a car with speed and stamina.

So no one was surprised when the company suddenly decided to go into stock-car racing in a big way. Some of the day's fastest drivers were soon seen making the circuits with cars whose sides were emblazoned "The Fabulous Hudson Hornet" in foot-high letters. Their speed records and victories kept recurring with such regularity that it was news when a Hornet *didn't* win 1st place. From the 160-mile stock-car race at Daytona Beach, early in the year, to Atlanta's 100-mile drag in November, the Number One slot always seemed to be reserved for the power-packed Hornets and their daredevil drivers.

The following year it was the same story. More than once—since there would usually be several Hornet entries—the cheering crowds saw them thundering down the home stretch to the finish line in a photo finish, placing 1st, 2nd, 3rd, and 4th over the rest of the field.

Naturally, the Hudson company's public relation people made the most of these victories in their news releases. Everybody who cared soon knew that the Hudson Hornet—winner of 45 stock-car races—was the undisputed national stock-car champion.

But some people, unfortunately, didn't seem to care. Sales began to taper off, from a high of 80,000 cars a year, down to 30,000, then even fewer. Things were not going well with Hudson.

Rumors that the company was about to join forces with another independent car manufacturer proved to be true. In 1954, Hudson and Nash merged to become what was hoped would make Detroit's Big Three the Big Four.

As for the "fabulous Hudson Hornet," it buzzed its last gasp and quietly expired in June, 1957.

1952 / *Buick Skylark*

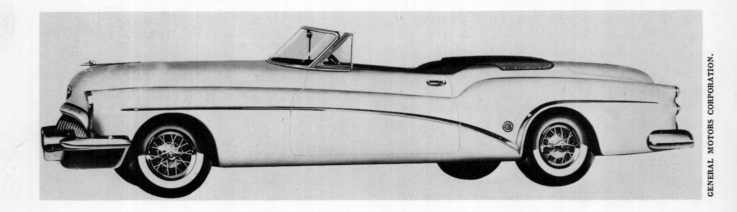

The summer of 1952 was a busy one in Flint, Michigan. The assembly lines were rolling and humming in preparation for the big event—the celebration of Buick's golden anniversary. The new cars, soon to be introduced for the 1953 model year, were heralded as "Buick's greatest cars in fifty great years." And they were.

Advance publicity releases bubbled with news of a mighty V-8 engine whose compression ratio had been boosted to 8.5 to 1—the highest in the industry. At the same time, Buick engineers had increased the cylinder bore to 4 inches and shortened the piston stroke to 3.2 inches. With a 4-barrel carburetor and an output of 188hp, the new V-8 was quite an engine.

The real headliner, though, was a brand-new Buick called the Skylark—a limited-edition convertible with a $5,000 price tag. Admittedly, that was a lot of money for a Buick. But it was a lot of car, too.

The heart of the Skylark was a standard 122-inch Roadmaster chassis, reworked to carry a special custom-built body of extraordinary beauty. First, the stylists dropped the beltline to give the car a long, rakish profile. Then they accented its road-hugging lowness with a graceful, flowing "swept-V" chrome strip. Wheel openings were circular, for full exposure of the smart imported wire wheels, each of which contained 40 individual chrome-plated wire spokes.

Even with the top up, the Skylark's overall height was 2 inches less than that of the regular production models. Its upholstery and trim, in soft-tanned genuine leather, recalled the elegance of prewar custom cars such as the Lincoln-Continental, while the flair of its modern styling contained a hint of the "personal" luxury cars that would soon be making their appearance on the American scene.

One detail that made the Skylark different from all other Buicks was the complete absence of the traditional "mouseholes" on the side of each front fender. For years, up until then, all Buicks had either 3, or 4, such chrome-rimmed openings in their front fenders. The engineers called them "venti-ports." As far as can be determined, no one had ever figured out what the use of them could be, but there they were—a styling trademark that was unmistakably "Buick." Luckily for the Skylark, its clean, uncluttered lines were not marred by the addition of "mouseholes."

Of all the 6 million automobiles produced by Buick during its first fifty years, this custom convertible was considered one of the loveliest. The company seemed to agree. With pardonable pride, it described the Skylark as "joyously free as the winged creature that gave it its name."

"Free"—for $5,000, that is.

1953/ *Corvette*

Not all dream cars come true. But this one did. From its modest beginning as a handcrafted 2-seater roadster, the Corvette was destined to become America's first and only true sports car—a position this marque still enjoys today.

In the early 1950s, there were about 100,000 sports cars registered in the United States, but all of them were expensive European imports. No one in this country was making small competition-cars on a production basis. The market seemed too limited.

One day, when General Motors' chief stylist was visiting his son over a college weekend, he met and chatted with some of the fellows on the campus who had been bitten by the sports-car bug. Most of them agreed they would be willing enough to switch over to an American-built sports car if somebody could build a real swinger at a price they could afford. "We'll give it a try," said stylist Harley Earl.

He tossed the assignment to his GM styling staff. To hold down development costs on the new car, the sketches and clay models were based on a standard Chevy convertible with a shortened wheelbase. The fiberglass mockup, completed in the spring of 1952, revealed a handsome, low-slung body with a sharply canted wrap-around windshield and a long hood sloping downward to a narrow, horizontal grille, in the best foreign sports-car tradition.

Elegantly trimmed, and painted oyster white, the Corvette-to-be was unveiled at a special showing for GM executives and won their enthusiastic approval.

The next job was to put together a chassis on which to hang the beautiful creation. In a rugged X-braced frame, the engineers mounted a Blue Flame 265-cubic-inch, 6-cylinder engine which had been souped-up with special cams, an aluminum manifold, and triple side-draft carbs—a combination that raised its output from 105 to 150hp.

When 8 prototypes of the car had been completed, the press was invited to drive them on the GM proving-ground test track. They created a sensation. Although their handling qualities were a bit disappointing, newsmen praised their lively acceleration and loved the muffled throb of their dual exhaust stacks.

Priced at $3,523—almost double what the company originally had in mind—the Corvette was officially introduced in January, 1953. At last, sports-car fans who could afford it had an American-built competition car that could hold its own with the imports.

In 1955, the 6-cylinder engine was replaced by a V-8, and in 1956 the car's performance was stepped up still more by a 225hp V-8. With the addition of a slick stick-shift gearbox and fuel injection in 1957, the Corvette became a car that could push the needle to 100mph in about 17 seconds. The later generation of Corvettes were called Stingrays.

1954/ *Kaiser Darrin*

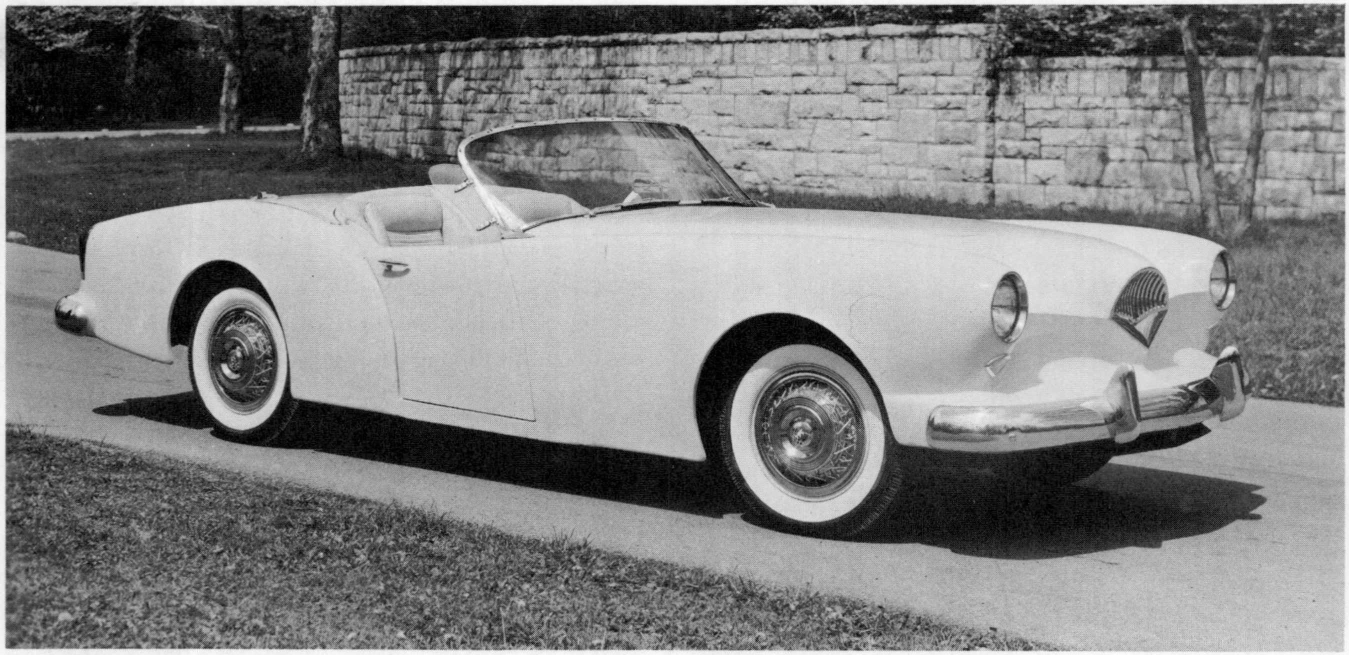

KAISER JEEP CORPORATION.

If ever a car was born to be a classic, it was this beautiful roadster. And if Kaiser-Frazer had only been able to put the car into production a year or so sooner than it did, the company's desperate last-ditch attempt at survival might have succeeded.

Oddly enough, the sporty speedster's direct ancestor was a gawky mini-sedan known as the Henry J, which had been named for the company's president, Henry J. Kaiser. The Henry J was a flop. The only good thing about the ill-fated car was its well-designed chassis and its lively F-head 6-cylinder Willys engine—a 90hp, 161-cubic-inch whirlwind. As for the Henry J's styling, the less said the better.

During the war, Henry Kaiser had proved himself a genius at mass-producing cargo ships, steel, and aluminum. But when it came to automobiles, he seemed to lack the magic touch. The public showed little enthusiasm for Kaiser-Frazer cars, including the Henry J.

Henry Kaiser was convinced that his ugly duckling could be transformed into a successful car if it were completely restyled. He called in the noted designer, Howard ("Dutch") Darrin, and asked him if he would create a new and glamorous body for the Henry J chassis. Darrin had recently returned to Hollywood after a long period as a coach-builder in Paris, where he had become renowned for his magnificent custom-built bodies for wealthy owners of such cars as the Rolls-Royce, Minerva, and Hispano-Suiza.

The celebrated designer agreed to take on the Henry J assignment if he were given a free hand, without interference from company stylists. Kaiser promised him this would be the case.

The result was a happy one. Darrin's sports convertible was breathtakingly beautiful. Officially, it was known as the KD-161: K for "Kaiser," D for "Darrin," and 161 for its engine displacement. Proving-ground tests proved it to be as nimble as it was good-looking. The KD-161 could accelerate from zero to 60mph in 16.3 seconds and had a top speed of 95mph on the straight.

The most remarkable feature of the car, in addition to its superb overall styling, was Darrin's masterstroke in designing doors that had no hinges. They opened by sliding forward on metal tracks into the front fenders. The idea was such an obvious improvement over conventional hinged doors and their hazards, it has been surprising that no other car manufacturer has since adopted it.

The Kaiser Darrin might well have become America's *second* successful sports car if fate had been kinder. But Kaiser's final days as an automobile man were at hand. Only several hundred KD-161's were ever produced.

1955 / *Continental Mark II*

William Clay Ford, the youngest grandson of the company's founder, still remembers the thrill of driving in Florida with his father, Edsel, in the original prototype of the 1939 custom-built Lincoln Continental. He was fourteen years old at the time.

When, as a young man, he became vice-president of the Ford Motor Company, he continued to have a warm spot in his heart for the very special car he had loved as a boy. A good many other people, too, remembered the old Lincoln Continental fondly. Over the years, letters kept coming to the company asking that the famous classic car be revived.

And so, in mid-1952, it was decided to form a special group of engineers and stylists within the company. The group was headed by young Mr. Ford. Its purpose, which was kept a well-guarded secret, was to design and build an exciting modern version of the "strictly continental" automobile that was so greatly admired a decade earlier. The car would be known as the Continental Mark II.

Four of the country's top car designers, together with the group's own stylists, were asked to submit drawings showing what they thought the new Continental should look like. Months later, when the drawings were completed, they were all displayed on the walls of the styling studio. No names were attached to the sketches, so no one knew which of the designers had drawn them.

Then, for several days, a jury of six Ford executives studied the sketches. There was never more than one man in the room at a time, and each was asked not to discuss his preference with the others. When the time came to count the votes, one set of sketches, and only one, received all six votes. William Clay Ford was naturally delighted to discover that the winning design had been submitted by his own styling group.

The dream began to take shape, from drawings to full-scale clay models. Then a number of hand-built prototypes were completed and put through all kinds of rugged tests. They were driven through snow, sleet, and mud, over scorching desert roads, up mountains, over railroad ties, through city traffic, and on the test track, where their big 285hp V-8 engines enabled them to clock a top speed of 118mph.

The new car made its formal entrance at the Paris Auto Show in October, 1955. Private showings followed in major U.S. cities. The Continental —longer, lower, and sleeker than ever—was back. During the next twenty months, 3,012 of them were produced; then this luxury line of cars was discontinued. For in the mid-1950s, fewer and fewer people felt they could afford to pay $10,000, even for a motorcar as distinguished as this. But the elegant Continental Mark II will never be forgotten. A decade after the last one was built, it was officially proclaimed a classic by the Classic Car Club of America.

1956 / *Thunderbird*

The early Thunderbirds were striking automobiles—and they still are, fifteen years or so after they first appeared. Parked alongside the curb, an original T-Bird is the kind of car that makes people exclaim with admiration, "They don't build them that way anymore!"

The clean, classic lines of the eager 2-seater carried out the same styling theme, in miniature, that made the stately Continental Mark II such a distinguished motorcar. The resemblance didn't just happen that way. The T-Bird was created in the same complex of Ford styling studios that designed the Mark II. Both cars were introduced in the same year—1955.

This Thunderbird is the distinctive 1956 model —the second T-Bird to be produced during the lifetime of the series. Its Continental wheel-mount was the only, but important, way in which it differed from the 1955 model. The third T-Bird, which appeared in 1957, had slightly canted tail fins. Aside from these differences, all three cars were the same.

This was the first time an American manufacturer had tried producing a small, luxurious automobile. Ford called it "a personal car." Priced at close to $3,000, it won the hearts of thousands of people who had been waiting for just such an American-built roadster.

Although its standard transmission was a synchromesh 4-speed gearbox with overdrive and floor-mounted stick, the plush little car could also be had with automatic transmission and such options as power brakes, power steering, power seats, and power windows.

The T-Bird engine was an 8-cylinder 90° "Y" with a displacement of 312 cubic inches. Since it developed well over 200hp, and the T-Bird weighed in at only slightly over 3,000 pounds, the car's favorable power/weight ratio enabled it, if pressed, to attain a top speed of 135mph.

It was naturally a nimble car on the road, but it was not a great success as a racing car. Its handling just couldn't be brought up to racing standards without changes that would have disqualified it for major track events. The Corvette, which was a true sports car, had a definite edge on the Thunderbird in this respect.

At the end of the 1957 model year, the Ford company decided to take the sporty little 2-seater out of production. T-Bird-lovers howled with dismay, even though the company announced that it *might* build them again sometime soon.

The 4-passenger 1958 Thunderbird, although bearing some resemblance to the original, turned out to be anything but. It was in a different category.

Less than 50,000 of the early T-Birds were sold in three years of production, while more than 53,000 of the new 1958 Thunderbirds were sold by the end of its first year. You can't argue with success. The only consolation is that the original T-Bird is now generally conceded to be a classic car.

1957/ Ford Fairlane

Once upon a time, back in the early 1950s, there was a mysterious car called the Mystere. You never saw it on the road and you undoubtedly never will. The Mystere was a "dream car," one of that special breed of automobiles that is designed and built behind the locked doors of some car manufacturer's experimental styling studio. Such a car is often known as an "X" car.

Sometimes an automobile company, seeking to learn the public's reaction to the styling and advanced engineering features of a new "X" car, exposes its experimental creation to as many people as possible. The car is put on display at national auto shows, the Paris Auto Show, at expositions and world fairs, where it can be viewed by several million people. Visitors are asked to write their opinion of the car on special cards, which they leave at the exhibit.

But in some cases, an "X" car is kept hush-hush and under wraps, seen and studied only by the company's own stylists, engineers, and top executives. If they all agree that the dream car has certain features they would like to incorporate in new models they are planning to produce, they borrow the ideas they want and discard the others.

When you look at the two photos showing the 1957 Ford Fairlane (*lower right*) and the "X" Mystere, it is easy to see how the Fairlane was inspired by this particular dream car.

Take the Mystere from the beltline down, refine its bold, flaring fins and decorative "V" chrome strip, reduce the size of the hooded headlamp enclosures, and you have a car that begins to look like the Fairlane.

Keep the slim hardtop roof line, the forward-slanting grille and windshield pillars, and reverse the light and dark areas of its two-tone paint job, and you almost have the Fairlane. Those massive wrap-around bumpers look good, so you keep them, too.

Then you stretch out the chassis 9 inches to make the car a long, sleek, road-hugger, and you put a 4-carb 212hp Thunderbird V-8 engine under its wide hood. Now you *do* have the Fairlane—one of the most beautiful high-performance cars that ever rolled off the Ford assembly lines.

1958 / *Edsel*

There is more than one way for a car to make news. This one did it by becoming the most costly mistake in automobile history. When it gave up the ghost, after only two years of production, the Ford Motor Company unhappily wrote it off as a $250 million loss.

The E-Car—which was its code name when it was still only an idea on the drawing board—is a car the company would like to forget. There was a jinx on it from the very start.

Even finding a good name for it turned into a fiasco. At first, they were going to call it the Edsel, after Henry Ford's son, who had died some years before. But Edsel's three sons did not like the idea of giving the unproved automobile their father's name.

So the search for a name went on. The company's advertising agency submitted an unwieldy list of 18,000 names. The list was cut to 6,000 names, and finally to 10. But no one could agree on any of them. As a last resort, the company asked the poet Marianne Moore to give it a try. She came up with such dillies as the Intelligent Bullet and the Utopian Turtletop.

At this point, a company official exclaimed, "This could go on forever. Let's go back to our original plan and call it the Edsel." The three Ford brothers reluctantly agreed.

The new car was formally introduced to the public in September, 1957, backed by the biggest publicity campaign since the loud hurrah for the old Model A, in 1928. People flocked to the showrooms to see it, and came away disappointed. They didn't think it lived up to its advance billing as the most sensational car ever built. Newsmen who had road-tested the car gave it only a so-so report on performance.

Above all, its styling left most people cold. Its most striking feature was a thin oval vertical grille, which bisected its full-width horizontal grille. Some wag remarked that the vertical grille reminded him of a horse collar. People were amused by the description. The Edsel soon became known as "the car with the horse collar on front." Its tail fins were sort of funny-looking, too. To some people they resembled stunted wings, or quizzical eyebrows.

The flop of the ill-fated Edsel was not due entirely to its off-beat styling. Just about the time of its introduction, the stock market took a nose dive. A recession was in the making. Hesitant to spend the money to buy a big "medium-priced" automobile, people were already swinging to the new so-called economy compacts. The Edsel just happened to be the wrong car at the wrong time.

There were people, of course, who loved the Edsel, and still do. Members of the Edsel Owners Club, all of whom keep their treasured cars in mint condition, insist that the Edsel was a far better car than most people realized. And it was.

1959 / *Cadillac*

This is the car that made styling history by coming out with the highest tail fins ever seen on an automobile. Almost all American cars had tail fins by 1959, but none were so awe-inspiring as these, which came to a sharp point at a height of 42.4 inches above the ground.

The story of the rise and fall of the great American tail fin goes back to the late 1940s, when Detroit's Big Three were racking their brains to come up with a styling change that would make their postwar vehicles irresistible to the buying public.

It all started when an Air Force colonel invited a friend of his to come out to a nearby airstrip to see an interesting new fighter plane. His friend happened to be the chief stylist at General Motors. The plane was the P-38, which had twin Allison engines, twin fuselages, and *twin tail fins*.

The unusual appearance of the fighter plane struck a spark in the stylist's creative mind. He asked if he might bring a couple of his designers out the next day to see it. The colonel agreed that they might come.

The designers, too, were impressed by the plane's unique lines. Perhaps this was the very clue they had been looking for—something that would give their cars a new look. Back at the studio, they turned out scads of sketches, most of which included tail fins. The result of their work first appeared on the 1948 Cadillac.

These early tail fins were modest things, scarcely more than upswept humps at the rear end of the fenders. But the public loved them. Cadillac sales rose. The next year, the fins grew bigger. So did Cadillac sales. The other car manufacturers sat up and took notice. Tail fins seemed to be the answer to what the public wanted, so they all got into the act.

From year to year during this period, tail fins took all shapes and forms. Some flared outward like the wings of a giant seagull. Others were sharply angular and vertical. Still others were built up in layers like a sandwich, with a center taillight where the hamburger should have been. One styling studio went so far overboard on its fin treatment that its car became a sort of flying wedge on wheels, its rear end bristling with pointed barbs like the gun turrets on an old B-24 bomber.

The idea seemed to be that if big fins sold cars, bigger fins would sell even more cars. The height of the styling fad was reached when the originator of the tail fin—Cadillac—introduced its 1959 models.

At that point, the stylists decided they had gone far enough. Fins could grow no higher. The only way was down. So, gradually, they became smaller and smaller. By 1965 no self-respecting tail fin could raise its head more than an inch or two above the rear-deck line. Then tail fins went the way of other styling fads and disappeared altogether.

133

1960 / *Corvair*

In late 1959, automobile newswriters hailed the coming of the 1960 Corvair as the beginning of a "revolution" in Detroit. At last, it seemed, one of the Big Three was bringing out a compact car. No longer would the small economy imports have the field all to themselves.

The Corvair was indeed a radical departure from standard American-built automobiles. To begin with, it had a peppy, air-cooled, aluminum, "pancake," 6-cylinder engine *mounted in the rear,* and was the first American car to have an independent suspension system for all 4 wheels.

It was an eager, nimble car, with bucket seats and a sporty flair. Only 51.3 inches high, it was 31 inches shorter than a standard Chevy, 13 inches narrower, and weighed 1,290 pounds less.

Whether equipped with the standard 95hp engine or a muscled-up mill with 4 carburetors, the Corvair, with its racy "4-on-the-floor" stick-shift, seemed to be the answer to thousands of motorists who wanted a sporty-looking economical car that was capable of flashy performance on the road. When the Corvair hit the showrooms, it created a mild sensation. Would it end up by being one of the smartest things Detroit had done in a decade, as some predicted, or a giant blunder? Nobody knew, but the car got off to a flying start. More than 235,000 people bought Corvairs during its first year

of production. The following year, sales reached 317,000, and they kept climbing until late 1965.

Then disaster struck. In a book called *Unsafe at Any Speed,* the author singled out the Corvair as a completely unstable car. He claimed—and cited instances of accidents on the highway to back up his claims—that its rear-mounted engine gave it the wrong weight distribution. It was not only tail-heavy, he said, but its 4-wheel suspension system tended to give it a "spin-out" force on curves like that of the end skater in a crack-the-whip line.

The following year, Corvair sales plummeted to 86,000, dipping to 12,977 in 1968. Corvair owners who had become involved in road accidents, for whatever reason at all, began to sue General Motors for damages. GM stoutly defended the car as being safe, and many loyal Corvair owners put "I Love My Corvair" stickers on their bumpers. But the death knell of the car had been sounded. On May 12, 1969, in the face of still dwindling sales, General Motors announced that it was taking the car out of production.

The keen, handsome Chevrolet Corvair will perhaps go down in history as "the car that was killed by a book." But at least 100,000 members of the Corvair Owners Club will probably never admit that the car they loved was anything but great.

1961 / *Lincoln Continental*

When the Continental Mark II was introduced in 1955, almost everyone agreed that it had succeeded nobly in recapturing the classic styling of the original Lincoln Continentals of the 1940s.

When the Mark II vanished, something must have happened in the hallowed halls of the Dearborn styling studios. The Continentals that followed it were not breathtakingly beautiful. Their lines were rather harsh and angular, with needless doodads and decorative chrome. Members of the exclusive Lincoln Continental Owners Club, and countless others who mourned the passing of the glorious old Continentals, took a dim view of the brash new pretenders.

The general lack of enthusiasm for the cars must have touched a sensitive nerve in Dearborn, for in 1961 the Ford Motor Company redeemed itself by bringing forth a motorcar that revived the Lincoln Continental tradition. Its sheer beauty and deliberate "elegant simplicity of styling" made it a truly worthy successor to the beloved Continentals of the past. All was forgiven.

The 4-door convertible, in particular, was a stunning motorcar. Lower, and more than a foot shorter than the ponderous-looking 1960 models, it had a minimum of brightwork—only a slim, stainless-steel molding to accent its handsome, clean-lined profile.

Considering that it was a big, luxurious automobile, the 1961 Lincoln Continental was a spectacular performer, too. It was powered by the biggest engine on the market—a 430-cubic-inch V-8 with a rating of 300hp. In a mere 40 seconds, it could move with a quiet hush from zero to a true 100mph, which came mighty close to being sports-car performance. The car had a comfortable, sure-footed cruising range of 80 to 90mph, and if you could find a legal stretch of highway where you could let it all out, the needle would move almost effortlessly up to the 120mph mark.

In spite of the healthy demand for the luxurious 1961 Lincoln Continentals, production of the expensive, limited-edition motorcar was held to less than 100 a day. Nearly half the time it took to build each car was spent in almost never-ending factory inspections, even if it meant delaying the completion of the car. Each engine was "hot-tested," then torn down. All its parts were closely inspected before the engine was reassembled and installed in the chassis. When completed, each car was given a 12-mile road test before receiving the chief inspector's O.K. for delivery.

Ford's Lincoln Continental division was understandably pleased, though not surprised, when its glamorous 1961 creation outsold all other luxury cars in the United States that year.

1962/ *Studebaker Avanti*

RAYMOND LOEWY.

The early 1960s found the 110-year-old Studebaker company in deepening trouble. It was no secret that its all-important automobile division was operating at a loss.

Studebaker's new president, energetic young Sherwood Egbert, was convinced that one answer to the problem was to bring out a completely new automobile—a car of such advanced design and exciting performance that public enthusiasm would be raised to fever pitch, resulting in sales that might help pull the company out of its crisis.

Inspired by his love for racing cars and certain European marques, Egbert drew some rough sketches of the kind of car he had in mind. Then he called in the famed industrial designer, Raymond Loewy, who had worked for Studebaker many times in the past.

Loewy was impressed by Egbert's suggestions and his natural flair for design. But he was startled when Studebaker's president said he wanted a prototype of the new car completed, not in eighteen months, but in two! Impossible? Perhaps. But Loewy said he would tackle the assignment, starting that day.

Taking two of his top automotive designers with him, he set up a crash work-program in an isolated rented house in the Mojave Desert, near his Palm Springs, California, home. In one short incredible week, the three designers had completed their drawings, "sweetened" them, and sculptured a $\frac{1}{8}$-scale clay model, which Loewy carried on his lap by jet plane back to South Bend.

The design, with a few minor changes, was approved. A selected team of stylists then got busy on the painstaking task of building a full-scale model. Thus began the countdown for the Avanti—a sleek, wedge-shaped creation that was unmistakably a classic-in-the-making.

Raymond Loewy's aerodynamic "Coke-bottle" design, coupled with the superb mechanical engineering of the car's chassis, resulted in a low 2-door "family sports car" of outstanding beauty and brilliant performance.

Equipped with a whopping 289-cubic-inch V-8 and an optional Paxton "blower," the Avanti was the first production car to have a built-in steel rollbar encircling its fully padded interior, as well as caliper disc brakes—2 safety features well suited to this thoroughbred package of power and speed.

On a trial run, the racing driver Andy Granatelli clocked a supercharged Avanti at 171mph from a standing start in 60.8 seconds. Then, traveling at 100mph, he slammed on his disc brakes and came to an unfaltering straight-line stop in 285 feet.

The Avanti, with its unique styling and heroic performance, was the sort of motorcar that might have saved Studebaker, had not the fortunes of the company ebbed so far. Word soon came that the company would cease to operate as an American auto maker and was shifting all car production to its Canadian plant.

Alas for the Avanti, another beautiful dream-car-that-might-have-been.

1963/ *Chrysler Gas Turbine Car*

How would you like it if someone came to your door and said, "Good morning. I'm from Chrysler. Would you be willing to drive one of our new experimental cars, just as if it were your own, for the next three months?"

That is exactly what happened to a man in Minneapolis on June 18, 1964—then to a man in Miami, and to a housewife in El Paso. By the end of 1965, Chrysler's experimental gas turbine cars had been placed in the hands of 200 other typical motorists, in forty-three different states. There were no strings attached, except that the company wanted to know what these motorists thought of the car after driving it for three months.

The idea of someday building a gas turbine car had been born back in 1945, when Chrysler was developing a new turboprop engine for navy aircraft. The engineers believed that if they could lick the problem of a turbine's tremendous thirst for fuel, and manage to cool off the intense heat of its exhaust gases, it might make an ideal automobile engine.

After completing their navy contract, the engineers worked for several years developing a similar engine for cars. In March, 1954, the first gas turbine in automobile history was installed in a Plymouth and road-tested. It worked, but there were many problems yet to be solved. One of them was to find new metal alloys that could withstand the fierce heat generated inside the engine's turbines.

Two years later, they came up with an improved, "second-generation" gas turbine. They installed it in another Plymouth and made a successful test run from New York to Los Angeles.

This experimental engine was followed five years later by a still better gas turbine, which was put through its paces on a 3,000-mile run through snowstorms, freezing rain, subzero temperatures, and blistering desert heat.

Finally, in May, 1963, the first Chrysler Gas Turbine car was ready for its official unveiling to the press at a private showing in New York City. It made big news. The company then launched the production of 50 more such cars, at the rate of 1 a week, to be put into the hands of typical motorists for testing.

The two-year test period, in which the cars were driven a total of more than a million miles, ended in January, 1966, when the last motorist, a Chicago woman, completed her three-month use of the car she had been loaned.

Most of the drivers were enthusiastic about the car. They liked its fast, smooth acceleration on the highway and what they called its wonderful "gliding sensation." Very few objected to the gentle whirring noise the turbines made.

Encouraged by the favorable reports that came in, Chrysler then decided to go ahead with the development of a new, "fifth-generation" turbine for possible use in the future.

Will most of tomorrow's cars be gas turbine automobiles? Nobody knows, yet. Not even Chrysler.

1964/ *Mustang*

Time, the weekly newsmagazine, usually devotes its cover to an important, newsworthy person. But in April, 1964, *Time*'s cover, as well as *Newsweek*'s, featured not a personality but an *automobile*—the new "1965" Ford Mustang, which had just been introduced in showrooms across the country.

The car was big news, obviously, to be thus honored, in the same week, by the two leading newsmagazines in the United States. In its inside ten-page story, *Time* called the new "animal" car one of the most heralded, attention-drawing cars in automobile history. The article went on to describe enthusiastically the car's long hood and short deck, its open-mouthed air scoop, its Ferrari flare, and its resemblance to European racing cars so admired by American sports-car buffs.

Everyone agreed: Ford had done it again. The company had created another landmark car, worthy to be numbered among the 5 others it had produced in its sixty-year history—the Model T, the Model A, the Lincoln-Continental, the Continental Mark II, and the '55 Thunderbird.

As in the case of other memorable cars, the Mustang was largely the inspiration of one man— Lee Anthony Iacocca. In his three years as manager of the company's Ford Division, this was the first car he could call his own, from blueprint through clay models to the production line.

The car was purposely designed to appeal to the youth market—young buyers who wanted exciting styling, "4-on-the-floor," bucket seats, and flashy performance. But the car made an instant hit with the older generation, too. Its formula was a happy combination of things that pleased everybody. It was a car demure enough to drive to church, stylish enough to park at the country club, and hot enough for the drag strip.

Anyone who wanted to spend more than the price of a standard Mustang could load it with just about every option Detroit could dream up—a choice of 7 different engines, 4 types of transmissions, 4 different wheel sizes, a high-performance axle ratio, 2 different suspension systems, custom wheel covers, a tachometer, and so on.

With all these things going for it, Mustang's sales hit a new record of 418,812 by the end of the first year and passed a million by March, 1966.

In the frenzy of planning, producing, and introducing the new car, one little detail escaped the notice of Lee Iacocca and his Ford associates, who apparently knew more about horsepower than they did about horseflesh. It was pointed out, too late for them to do anything about it, that the galloping steed adorning the grille of the car seemed to be running in the wrong direction. U.S. racehorses always run in the traditional counterclockwise direction, but Ford's mustang had bolted off in the other direction, like a runaway. Ford's answer, of course, was that the Mustang was a runaway car, designed to give Chevy, Buick, Olds, and Pontiac a run for their money. Which it did.

143

1965 / *Barracuda*

When the 1965 Plymouth Barracuda made its debut, one road-and-track expert was unkind enough to say that it was just a mild-mannered fish and not the ferocious slasher its name suggested. But when race-minded Plymouth stepped up its power package with an optional 235hp, 4-carb V-8 engine, there was no denying that it was now a lively performer, as well as one of the sleekest and most handsome of the 1965 "specialty" cars.

The Barracuda made no claim to being a true sports car. It was simply a sporty car. But it had many GT styling touches and engineering features that almost put it into the sports-car category. With its Formula S options, it gave the owner such goodies as exposed lug-nut wheel covers, a tachometer, a flip-open standard pit-stop gas cap on the fuel tank, heavy-duty suspension and sway bar, front-wheel disc brakes, and fast-ratio manual steering, plus bucket seats and "4-on-the-floor." The final racy touch was a broad rallye stripe running the length of the body, from hood to rear deck—a subtle reminder that while the Barracuda was not a competition car in the strictest sense, it was a car that could give a good account of itself if pressed.

It was an excellent road car, too, with brisk acceleration and good cornering qualities. Designed as Plymouth's bid to capture the favor of young-at-heart motorists, it clearly offered more excitement and glamor than Detroit's standard product.

Although it was a 5-seater, the Barracuda could be converted into a 2-seater with a 7-foot cargo space in back simply by folding down the bench-type rear seat—a feature that appealed to golfers and sportsmen as well as their grocery-toting wives.

Two years after the introduction of the car, Plymouth engineers boosted its performance still further with an optional competition-type 275hp V-8 that could move the car from zero to 60mph in an amazing 5.9 seconds, and at a top speed of 125mph. When this happened, the company proudly sent out word that the souped-up Barracuda "could cut a better lap-time anywhere from Watkins Glen to Waterford Hills." There were few to dispute it.

But by this time, the Barracuda's position had become secure, not only with the heavy-footed gentry but with a lot of people who had heard of Watkins Glen only because of its scenic gorge and waterfalls and who couldn't have cared less about its famed annual Grand Prix race meets.

The rakish sports-compact was rated tops, especially by younger buyers, with full membership in the popular "animal club" of American cars.

1966/ *Olds Toronado*

The principle of front-wheel drive is as old as the automobile itself. In 1879, the American inventor George Selden applied for a patent on a design for a front-driven gas buggy. But other pioneer automobile builders shied away from the idea of applying power directly to the front wheels of their horseless carriages. It involved too many mechanical problems. So FWD was pretty much forgotten.

Citroën of France, however, has been producing front-driven automobiles for more than thirty years with great success. In this country, the distinctive Cord 810, introduced in 1935, was the first front-wheel-drive car to win popular approval. But the Cord soon vanished from the scene, mourned as a noble experiment that deserved a better fate.

For a long time after the disappearance of the Cord, the idea of pulling an automobile forward by its front wheels continued to haunt many an automotive engineer. It had advantages that made a lot of sense.

The idea kept simmering and finally came to life again. In 1966, after a long hush-hush period of development, General Motors announced the introduction of "a totally new kind of car." It was, of course, the front-wheel-drive Olds Toronado.

Actually, GM engineers had spent seven years in the step-by-step development of the Toronado's chassis and drive-train units. It wasn't until the last three of those years, when the major engineering problems had been solved, that the Oldsmobile stylists were given the green light to start designing a body to put on the chassis.

When the public got its first glimpse of the Toronado, some press reporters called it the most distinguished American automobile since Gordon Buehrig's stunning Cord 810. Like the Cord, it was a front-driven automobile with all its inner workings and drive-train units contained in one big neat package up front. So the stylists gleefully covered the package with a hood 6 feet long—almost $\frac{1}{3}$ as long as the car itself. This frontal treatment, combined with its low profile and bold wheel openings, set the Toronado apart from conventional automobiles at a glance. The beautiful beast must have made the little Merry Oldsmobile of 1901 whirl in its grave with envy!

In later models, refinements were made in the design of the grille, and its original 425-cubic-inch V-8 was boosted to 455, with an output of 375hp at 4,600rpm.

Impressed by motorists' enthusiasm for the Toronado—and especially its surefooted handling qualities on the road—Cadillac jumped onto the bandwagon a year later by bringing out its elegant front-wheel-drive Eldorado.

It, too, was a successful car, but other manufacturers did not indicate they had any intention of switching from conventional rear-wheel drive to FWD automobiles.

1967 / *Javelin*

It was no secret, in early 1967, that the big American Motors Corporation was operating at a heavy loss and sales were continuing their downward skid. It was a puzzling situation, for the company was producing automobiles that were known to be excellent, and they were reasonably priced. But clearly, something had to be done to turn the tide.

That summer, word began to spread that American Motors was coming up with a new car that would be a winner. It just might be the answer.

Everyone hoped so, including the top management of Detroit's Big Three. For it would have been considered a calamity, for the industry and the economy, if the nation's fourth largest automobile manufacturer should lose its fight for survival in the prosperous 1960s, as did so many fine old auto companies during the grim depression years of the 1930s.

On September 26, 1967, the sporty new Javelin went on display in American Motors showrooms across the country. It was a 2-door hardtop with a racy look that stylist Richard Teague was counting on to change the rather stodgy, workaday image of previous AM cars. No doubt about it, the new car was a swinger.

When the public, and especially youthful showroom tire-kickers, viewed the Javelin, they liked what they saw. Newsmen called it "a man's car."

One expert who test-drove it reported: "When you put the car in motion, you'd better be prepared for business. It asks for only one kind of treatment: hard, rugged driving."

In aiming for a share of the "sporty car" market, it seemed that American Motors had hit the target squarely with its javelin. The car had great style, with a long hood and short, fast-line rear deck. It was low and sleek—a real road-hugger.

The car came in 2 models—a standard Javelin and an even more glamorous SST. The basic power plant for both models was a 145hp 6-cylinder engine. But optional V-8's could be had, too, including a high-performance 4-carb package with a displacement of 343 cubic inches and a 280hp rating at 4800rpm.

The car deserved to be a success, and it was. In 1968, its first full year of production, 56,462 Javelins were built and sold, 1,320 of them going into the export market for eager overseas buyers who knew a good thing when they saw it.

Best of all, American Motors happily announced a net profit of close to $12 million that year, instead of showing an operating loss of over $75 million, as it had in the previous year. Perhaps the jaunty Javelin should not be given the entire credit for the upswing in the company's fortunes, but it did, at least, mark the turning point.

1968 / *Continental Mark III*

FORD MOTOR COMPANY.

If you were writing the story of the classic Continentals built by the Ford Motor Company, you would of course include this glamorous 1968 luxury car, which was introduced at a special press preview in December, 1967.

All of the Continentals ever built were known as "personal" motorcars, inspired by one individual and designed to look the way that person thought it should look. Edsel Ford had his special Lincoln Continental; his son Bill's special love was the Continental Mark II; and in the 1968 model year, the beautiful Mark III came on the scene, a special motorcar created under the personal direction of Henry Ford II, the present head of the company, to carry on the tradition of the earlier "strictly continental" motorcars. So, it seems, as long as there is "a Ford at Ford," there will always be a "personal" custom-built Continental.

It is interesting to compare all three cars—the original Lincoln Continental (*upper left*), the Mark II (*upper right*), and the Mark III (*foreground*)— and see how much their basic styling has in common. They all, of course, have a continental wheelmount, in one form or another. All three have pleasingly low profiles, with a close-coupled passenger compartment and a relatively short rear deck. The sleek Mark III, with a height of only 52.9 inches, is a true road-hugger. Its hood, with a length of slightly more than 6 feet, is the longest of any American car on the road. But its most distinctive feature is the squared vertical grille, which is not unlike that of the Rolls-Royce.

Back in February, 1966, when Ford company executives were looking over the various sets of sketches for the latest Continental, Henry Ford II pointed to one of them and said, *"That's* the car I'd like to drive home." And he did, eventually, for that was the design that was put into the works, from clay models to prototypes and the almost endless series of tests on road and track.

The Mark III, powered by a husky 365hp V-8, was a nimble car that moved with the effortless ease of a sports car. In track tests, it was clocked from zero to 60mph in less than 10 seconds, which isn't bad for a luxurious 4-passenger coupé. Since most manufacturers seldom publicize top-speed figures, it was enough to say that it was no trick at all to push the Mark III's needle into the 100 segment of the gauge.

The 1,000 members of the Lincoln Continental Owners Club, who spend countless hours keeping their beloved cars in mint condition, seem to agree that the stately Mark III was a worthy successor to the legendary Lincoln Continental of the 1940s and the 1955 Mark II. Only time will tell whether it will someday join them as a true and official American classic.

1969 / *Camaro Z-28*

Chevrolet introduced its spirited Camaro Z-28 with the pardonable boast: "If you want more car than this, you'll have to go to the Corvette Stingray, or maybe the Indianapolis 500." They had a point. The Z-28 was anything but a sedate family sedan. It was about as close as you could come to a pure sports car and still get a rear seat and trunk in the deal.

The Z-28 emblem on the car's narrow grille stood for the optional power package with which a sports-minded driver could muscle-up his standard Camaro, at extra cost, to bring it up to (but not beyond) strict Trans-Am racing specifications. The result was a $4,000 track performer with a quarter-mile time of 15 seconds—a feat it accomplished due to its ability to wind up to 96mph from a standing start. On extended track tests, it clocked an official 137mph. This beefed-up Camaro, with its ground-hugging fat tires, was definitely not a street car.

Sports-car buffs were enthusiastic, if perhaps a little surprised, at Chevrolet's offering them such a demon of a car. For the company, unlike Ford and Chrysler, had officially abandoned attempts to use race-circuit publicity as a means of adding glamour and sales-appeal to its various lines of standard automobiles.

Ford was quick to accept the challenge of the Z-28 by bringing out a revamped version of the Mustang which it dubbed the Boss 302. The two competing cars were similar in styling and their performance records were almost identical. Both were powered by 302 cubic-inch V-8's with a 4 x 3 bore and stroke. The Camaro's engine developed 290hp at 5,800rpm. So did the engine of the Boss 302. Their quarter-mile time and top speed on the track were equally—and exactly—impressive: 15 seconds and 137mph. Both had power-assisted disc brakes. Even their wheelbases were the same: 108 inches.

The Camaro Z-28, being the first of the 2 cars to whiz onto the scene, gained instant recognition for its lively, sporty styling, its acceleration, its quick-ratio steering, and superb handling qualities. The fact that it could out-perform most sports cars then on the road was a compliment to the engineers who had managed to transform what was simply a nifty-looking coupé into a mean, snarling "king-of-the-track" in its class.

Full wheel openings, a stubby rear end and air-spoiler, a 4-speed transmission with a floor-mounted shift-stick, plus bold rallye striping on hood and rear deck, left no doubt that the Z-28 was an eager car with big ideas.

So, with the power-packed Camaro and the not-to-be-outdone Boss 302 vying with each other to give America the super high-performance cars it wanted, the 1969 Trans-Am races were bound to be an even more hotly contested event than in the previous year, when race driver Mark Donohue piloted his 1968 Camaro to a runaway victory in the T-A series.

1970/ Maverick

Back in 1955, a dark cloud no bigger than a Volkswagen appeared over the Detroit horizon. That year, for some reason or another, 50,000 people who had always driven American-built automobiles switched over to the little imported "beetle." The Big Three, busily rolling new cars off their assembly lines by the millions, were not unduly alarmed. "It's just a fad," they said. "They'll never sell enough of them to really hurt us."

But the cloud grew bigger. With each passing year, foreign imports kept nibbling bigger bites from Detroit's share of the American automobile market. Before long, the sale of imported cars had swelled to an unbelievable 10 percent of all automobiles sold in the United States. More than half a million of these foreign cars were Volkswagens. Another 127,696 of them were Japanese cars. It was obvious to everybody, by this time, that simply ignoring the small imported cars wouldn't make them go away.

American auto makers had tried to stem the flood of foreign "economy" cars about ten years before by introducing their own so-called compact cars. But with each succeeding model year, the "compacts" kept getting bigger and bigger, and soon became too costly to compete with the little VW and other "sub-compacts" from overseas.

Thus it was welcome news when Ford announced, in April of 1969, that it was bringing out a new kind of small car to combat the invasion of German "beetles" and Japanese Datsuns and Toyotas. The car, developed over a period of three years at a cost of $71 million, was named the Maverick.

It was a 2-door, 4-passenger sedan—a sporty, cut-down version of the popular Ford hardtop. While its overall length was 179.4 inches (19 inches longer than the VW), it could U-turn in a tight 36½-foot circle, beating the VW's turning circle by 6 inches. Powered by a peppy 6-cylinder engine, its 105hp was ample to give it a turnpike cruising speed of 70mph. Its gas economy was quoted at 22 miles per gallon, only 3 less than the VW's claim of 25 miles per gallon.

The 1970 Maverick, with a price tag of $1,995, was inexpensive enough to appeal to people of limited means, and as a third car for 2-car families. Ford announced there would be no yearly styling changes. The design, they said, was "locked-in," at least until 1972. To attract young buyers, the car was offered in a choice of psychedelic colors bearing such far-out names as Freudian Gilt, Thanks Vermillion, Original Cinnamon, and Hulla-Blue.

Some car experts thought the Maverick wasn't small enough, or priced low enough, to make much of a dent on foreign-car sales. Possibly Ford shared these misgivings, because even as the Maverick was announced, there were rumors of a still smaller, less expensive car nearing completion in the company's development laboratories.

Are the Maverick, and similar Detroit compacts that followed it, causing sleepless nights in Wolfsburg and Yokohama? Perhaps. But again, maybe not.

Index